FRONTLINES

FRANK

THE *WIK* DEBATE

ITS IMPACT ON ABORIGINES, PASTORALISTS AND MINERS

UNSW PRESS

Other books by Frank Brennan

Too Much Order With Too Little Law
Finding Common Ground (editor)
Land Rights Queensland Style
Sharing the Country
Reconciling Our Differences (editor)
One Land One Nation
Legislating Liberty

A UNSW Press book

Published by
University of New South Wales Press Ltd
University of New South Wales
Sydney 2052 Australia

First published 1998

National Library of Australia
Cataloguing-in-Publication entry:

Brennan, Frank, 1954– .
The Wik debate: its impact on aborigines, pastoralists and miners.

Bibliography.
ISBN 0 86840 409 8.

1. Australia. Native Title Act 1993. 2. Australia. High Court. Wik peoples v. State of Queensland and others. 3. Native title. 4. Land tenure—Law and legislation—Australia. I. Title.(Series: Frontlines (Sydney)).

346.940432

Printed by Griffin Press Pty Ltd, Adelaide

CONTENTS

PREFACE

Since the High Court's *Wik* decision, I have travelled the length and breadth of Australia meeting with Aboriginal groups and their supporters, pastoralists and church groups. Even when emotions have been high, the hospitality has been very Australian, as we have searched for solutions. I acknowledge all those persons who arranged meetings and provided transport and accommodation.

I am especially grateful to the pastoralist who urged me to return to my church and say prayers. He clarified my thinking. An issue as complex as *Wik* cannot be left only to the stakeholders. It is unlikely to be resolved by prayer alone. There is probably a place for honest brokers. Being neither a native title holder, miner nor pastoralist, I have been privileged to participate in the debate. I thank the stakeholders and politicians who have opened their doors to me.

A High Court decision on native title decided by the barest majority with controversial reasoning, presented to a new government unsympathetic to any expansion of native title rights, and considered by a Senate in which a Tasmanian Independent has the balance of power, is a potent political cocktail. I trust this book contributes to a better understanding and a resolution of the issue for the good of all Australians.

I thank the Reshaping Australian Institutions Project at the Australian National University for the opportunity to step back and write. I thank the Australian Institute of Jesuit Studies and Uniya, the Jesuit Social Justice Centre, for their support.

ABBREVIATIONS

ALP	Australian Labor Party
AMEC	Association of Mining and Exploration Companies
ATSIC	Aboriginal and Torres Strait Islander Commission
MCA	Minerals Council of Australia
NTA	*Native Title Act 1993*
NFF	National Farmers Federation
NIWG	National Indigenous Working Group on Native Title
NNTT	National Native Title Tribunal
QC	Queen's Counsel
RDA	*Racial Discrimination Act 1975*

INTRODUCTION

The six colonies established on the Australian continent were the only colonies in the history of British colonialism founded without any recognition of the rights of the indigenous peoples to their lands and without any treaties. In 1971, a single judge of the Northern Territory Supreme Court decided that British law did not recognise the communal rights in land which were undoubtedly enjoyed by Aborigines before colonisation and that any rights would be extinguished by the mere assertion of British sovereignty over the territory. It was as if Australia were *terra nullius*.

The only rights to land enjoyed by Aborigines and Torres Strait Islanders were rights granted under land rights legislation. It was not until the *Mabo* case in 1992 that Australia's highest court, the High Court of Australia, was required to determine issues about native title. Since *Mabo*, the nation has been wrestling with a two hundred year history infected by the *terra nullius* mindset. Despite the wholesale dispossession that occurred, some indigenous Australians have maintained the native title rights of their ancestors. Those rights now have to be respected whenever new developments are to occur on the land. Governments and developers need to know with whom to deal. Aboriginal groups need to be able to resolve conflicting claims.

Native title now involves all levels of government in Australia. It involves the courts as well as our parliaments. For some developers, native title is simply a land management issue. For some indigenous groups, it is the symbolic bedrock of a new recognition and accommodation of indigenous aspirations and perspectives in the life of the nation. The High Court's *Wik* decision in 1996 clarified that native title was not restricted to vacant crown land. It could survive and perhaps even revive on land to which other citizens had been granted rights.

Between *Mabo* and *Wik*, there were changes to the composition of the High Court. *Wik* was decided by the narrowest margin of four–three. There was then a change of government in Canberra. These legal and political changes affected the responses made to the new questions emerging about native title. Not all questions have been resolved. There will be more court cases heard by a newly constituted High Court. Only two of the seven judges who decided *Mabo* are still on the bench. Though the High Court will continue to uphold the *Mabo* decision, it is likely to confine the *Wik* decision to its facts, restricting the possibility of native title surviving on other tenures or reviving on lands subject to crown grant or dedicated and used for public purposes.

It is common ground that complications arising from court decisions about native title are not to be resolved by parliaments legislating a wholesale extinguishment of native title. Even in the name of workability and certainty, native title holders should not be treated unfairly. Native title rights should be treated in a non-discriminatory way. Parliaments are entitled to change the law set down by the courts but they have to act within constitutional power and they should respect people's property rights. Native title holders should have some say about new developments occurring on their traditional lands.

There are still many areas of disagreement. If courts are free to develop the law of native title, parliaments may want to override those developments in the national interest. While some politicians are happy to expand the scope of native title rights, treating them as if they were freehold property rights and granting a right to negotiate with developers, others claim a mandate for confining native title rights to the bare minimum recognised by the courts. Former Prime Minister Keating wanted to avoid further litigation and even more complex legislation by negotiating an agreed outcome with indigenous leaders. Prime Minister Howard wanted a return to certainty by limiting the entitlements of native title holders to what miners and pastoralists found acceptable and leaving land management issues to the States. While all reasonable participants in the debate have insisted that native title rights be treated in a non-discriminatory way, there has been disagreement about how best this can be achieved while still ensuring a certain and workable outcome for all stakeholders. There have been very complex discussions about the *Racial Discrimination Act 1975 (RDA)* which, for some, is the Australian bill of rights, and for others, a Commonwealth law to be superseded by new Commonwealth laws whenever the need arises. On the Labor side of politics, the protection of Aboriginal rights is usually seen as a Commonwealth responsibility. On the other side of politics, it is more often seen as a matter for the States. The intense debate about federal–state responsibilities and about the role of courts and parliaments has taken place in a hostile environment marked by unprecedented attacks by governments on the High Court and even the churches.

I have been an active participant in the national debate on these complex issues. Though my sympathies are with Aborigines, my perspective on the complex legal and political issues has not always coincided with that of the indigenous leadership. In the lead-up to the second Senate debate on *Wik*, Aden Ridgeway, senior member of the National Indigenous Working Group (NIWG), wrote to the *Sydney Morning Herald*:

> There is no doubt that Fr Brennan has immense respect and affection amongst Aboriginal people throughout the country. More significantly, he is widely listened to by Australians generally because he is believed to speak for Aboriginal people. This has created a desperately difficult dilemma for indigenous leaders. Fr Brennan's support and advocacy are much needed; but where he takes a stand which differs from that of Aboriginal people themselves, especially over difficult issues of political judgment, the very fact that he is believed by the general community to speak for Aborigines suggests that he should be silent on such topics.

Another NIWG member, Geoff Clarke, was less flattering: 'I think the problem with Father Frank's proposal and advocacy is that there's no more lost tribes to represent, and indigenous people could quite adequately represent their views on issues that affect them'. Happily a week later, both parties agreed that the time for silence had passed. Prior to the third Senate debate, I publicly advocated a compromise. I did not participate in the discussions between Mr Howard and Senator Harradine and their lawyers. I did endorse the compromise when I was informed of its key components.

Not being a stakeholder, I present the case for Aborigines, pastoralists and miners, attempting to hold in balance the principles of justice, workability and certainty, and knowing that the account will not bring complete satisfaction to any stakeholder. This book traces the legal developments and political manoeuvring since *Mabo*, through the intrigue of Keating's *Native Title Act*, the complexity of the High Court's *Wik* decision and the exhausting drama of Howard's Ten Point Plan, culminating in the Howard–Harradine compromise which was passed into law on 8 July 1998, 18 months after the *Wik* decision.

1 THE UNANSWERED QUESTIONS ARISING AFTER *MABO* 1992

Eddie Mabo commenced his court case in 1982 claiming rights to his traditional land on the island of Mer in the Torres Strait. Until then land rights had been a political issue rather than a legal one. Land rights had previously been granted by various governments and parliaments to indigenous communities. Eddie Mabo and his fellow claimants were the first indigenous Australians to succeed in the courts, establishing that their native title rights were recognised by the courts, even though no government or parliament had taken action to recognise their rights. Until the *Mabo* case, it was presumed that Aborigines and Torres Strait Islanders had no rights to land other than those rights granted to them by the colonising power. The presumption was that the land was *terra nullius*, being 'practically unoccupied' at the time of British 'settlement', when the sovereignty of the Crown was asserted over the territory in which indigenous Australians happened to be living. By succeeding in the courts, indigenous Australians overthrew the myth and challenged the thinking of *terra nullius*. But that thinking has remained part of the non-indigenous Australian community's response to the *Mabo* judgment.

The Queensland Government defended the *Mabo* case in the High Court. That government's first defence was a classic *terra nullius* response. Preparing for the case, the Queensland government presumed that the courts could find that some native title rights survived the assertion of British sovereignty and had survived until the present. The government drafted legislation for passage through the Queensland Parliament. The *Queensland Coastal Islands Declaratory Act 1985* purported simply to extinguish any surviving native title rights without payment of compensation. The extinguishment was to be backdated to 1879 when the Torres Strait Islands were incorporated into the colony of Queensland.

In 1988, the High Court of Australia ruled that this retrospective extinguishment of any surviving native title was contrary to the *Racial Discrimination Act 1975* (*RDA*), which had been passed by the Commonwealth Parliament as a domestic implementation of the *International Convention on the Elimination of All Forms of Racial Discrimination*. In 1992 the *Mabo* proceedings returned to the seven justices of the High Court who, with only Justice Dawson dissenting, ruled that native title was recognised by the common law, which is the law developed by the judges to resolve disputes brought by parties before the court. The court accepted that indigenous communities had their own systems of land law prior to the arrival of the colonisers. Members of those communities retained their rights and interests in their traditional lands unless and until the new sovereign took action inconsistent with the continuation of those rights and interests. Native title would usually be extinguished when the Crown granted the land to another person who then had the right to exclude native title holders from access to the land. It could also be extinguished by the government appropriating the land to its own use or for some public purpose. Much of the Australian land mass, especially in Western Australia, was still vacant crown land which had never been allocated to others or used by the Crown. Native title could still exist on such areas.

The plaintiffs in *Mabo* relied on developments in the Canadian courts and submitted that the State of Queensland was under a fiduciary duty to protect the ongoing native title rights of the indigenous people. A fiduciary duty is a duty of trust owed by one party to another when the first party is in a position of influence, having both the power and the obligation to look after the interests of the second party. If this duty of trust existed, native title holders would have been able to seek court assistance to restrain future interference with native title by a State government. Also, they may have been able to question the validity of past dealings with native title land. This argument was not taken up by any of the judges except Justice Toohey. He thought that the power of the Crown to extinguish native title gave rise to a fiduciary obligation. However he did concede that the existence of the obligation on the Crown could not limit the power of a State parliament which could then authorise a State government to extinguish native title.

The bench went to great lengths to avoid spelling out the content of native title rights. The detail of those rights would depend on the local law and custom of the indigenous community. One group's native title rights may simply be the entitlement to travel across the land periodically for the gathering of bush tucker. Another group's rights might include the right to exclusive and constant occupation and use of the land. In the absence of any fiduciary duty, State parliaments were at liberty to extinguish native title and to authorise State government interference with native title. Prior to 1975 there was no limitation on a State's power to take away native title. The cornerstone of the High Court's jurisprudence of native title was the *RDA* which has featured in every debate about native title ever since.

Because the *RDA* is a valid Commonwealth law, any State law or practice after 1975 has to be non-discriminatory. How could a State government be sure it was treating native title holders in a non-discriminatory way? The only shorthand guarantee would have been for State governments to deal with native title holders in the same way that they dealt with ordinary titleholders such as those who own a freehold block granted by the Crown. If State governments were to deal with native title holders in a different way, they would have to show that the difference related to the different form of title and was not discriminatory.

The major unresolved question in *Mabo* was whether or not the grant of a pastoral lease extinguished native title. Pastoral leases were a unique Australian form of title developed in the nineteenth century to meet the needs of those squatters wanting to operate vast sheep and cattle runs outside the more closely settled areas that had been opened for selection. There were, of course, no pastoral leases issued in the Torres Strait Islands. However, in the course of *Mabo*, some judges had cause to comment on a lease which had been granted in 1931 for the conduct of a sardine factory. That lease contained a reservation in favour of the natives:

> The Lessees shall not in any way obstruct or interfere with the use by the Murray Island natives of their tribal gardens and plantation of the leased land. The Lessees shall not in any way obstruct or interfere with the operations of the Murray Island natives who fish around the reefs adjacent to the leased land for Beche-de-mer, Trochus, etc.

Justices Brennan, Mason and McHugh concluded that the traditional rights and interests of the Meriam people were extinguished on the leased area despite the reservations stated in the lease. By granting the lease, the Crown had granted the lessee the right of possession. Once the lease expired the full interest in the land reverted to the Crown. Any right of access for the natives would be set down in the lease. No right of access to the leased area would any longer be derived from Meriam laws and customs. Justice Dawson, who dissented on the basis that native title was not recognised by the common law, would have agreed with this reasoning. Justices Deane and Gaudron were of the opposite view. They thought the lease recognised and protected the rights of the Murray Islanders. If the lease expired, the rights of Murray Islanders under common law native title would continue. Justice Toohey, the sixth member of the majority, did not find it necessary to proffer a view but his reasoning would have supported the proposition that native title would continue despite the grant of such a lease.

In the light of the reasoning of the judges about native title and the sardine factory lease, it is reasonable to assume that the High Court, as then constituted in 1992, would have decided four–three that any form of lease including a pastoral lease would have extinguished native title. This would have been the case even if the lease permitted some ongoing access to the land by the local indigenous population.

While negotiations and discussions were proceeding about the *Native Title Act* in 1993, the Cape York Land Council, which had been consulting with traditional owners on the west coast of Cape York, decided to commence a test case in the courts which would investigate the limits of these uncertainties. The case would relate to land subject to bauxite mining leases granted to Comalco by the Queensland government in 1957 and therefore prior to the *RDA*. It would also cover areas subject to pastoral leases, some of which had expired. The details of the case were announced in July 1993 when Comalco was trying to secure international financing for a new smelter project. There were threats that the company would require the Queensland government to pass special legislation ensuring the security of Comalco's titles.

There was never any real prospect that the claims relating to invalidity of the mining leases would succeed. The Comalco leases were granted pursuant to agreements between the company and government. Those agreements were then the subject of special Acts of the Queensland Parliament passed in 1957, which provided that each agreement was to 'have the force of law as though the Agreement were an enactment' of the parliament. If those leases and agreements could have been struck down by the courts, so too could any lease or agreement made before or after the passage of the *RDA*. The Aboriginal claimants had no hope of succeeding on the argument about fiduciary duty. The pastoral lease issue was expected to be a more close run thing.

2 THE PURPOSE OF THE *NATIVE TITLE ACT 1993*

In the wake of the *Mabo* decision, government and industry faced two major problems. First there was doubt about the validity of Crown grants and permits for land use granted since 1975. Second, there was doubt about the appropriate way to proceed with land development applications in future. Native title extinguished before 1975 was lost forever and those native title holders who had lost their rights had no legal entitlement to compensation. If native title had survived on an area of land between 1788 and 1975, State governments and State parliaments would thereafter have to deal with the land in a manner consistent with the *RDA*. Effectively, this meant that land management from 1975 and into the future had to be administered in a non-discriminatory way unless the Commonwealth Parliament were to interfere with the *RDA*. And that was just not an option.

Shortly after the *Mabo* decision, Prime Minister Keating was apprised of these problems and appreciated the need for a political solution rather than ongoing litigation in the courts. So while the Cape York Land Council was preparing the *Wik* case, Keating started a round of consultations, anxious to broker a deal acceptable to all stakeholders. He accepted the need for a federal scheme of Commonwealth and State legislation validating all land dealings since 1975. There was no need for the scheme to affect pre-1975 land dealings because their validity was not affected by the High Court's findings about native title. Any indigenous Australians whose native title rights had been affected by post-1975 land dealings would be entitled to compensation. Aboriginal leaders knew they would have to accept a validation regime. The only alternative would have been protracted uncertainty about land titles while courts decided disputed questions on a case by case basis. Though agreeable to the inevitable, these leaders understandably wanted something in return. They wanted to ensure that the political process had moved with the legal times, ruling out a *terra nullius* resolution of outstanding concerns.

Keating wanted an outcome in the ballpark of certainty, workability and fairness. In the native title debate, these have been the three key principles. The disagreements have usually been about which principle is to enjoy priority. From the Aboriginal perspective, certainty and workability are often a foil for further interference with native title rights. They are the modern acceptable language of those who have not yet abandoned the *terra nullius* mindset.

Validation of past actions was never a major political problem. A non-discriminatory regime for future actions on native title was the real headache. The problem was highlighted by the situation in Western Australia where almost half the land mass had never been alienated or appropriated for anything other than Aboriginal use and occupation. Native title could still exist on such land. If challenged, Aboriginal claimants would need to be able to establish that they had maintained their traditional connection with the land, having continued both to acknowledge their own system of laws and to observe their customs as far as practicable. The problem was highlighted by the case of a miner wanting access to the Gibson Desert for mineral exploration. Prior to *Mabo,* the miner would simply deal with a public servant in Perth and obtain the necessary exploration permit. After *Mabo*, the public servant could not automatically issue such a permit. The State government would first of all need to be satisfied that there were no native title holders or that the native title holders had been treated in a non-discriminatory way. There was no register of native title holders. The State officials would throw the responsibility back to the miner who would claim that he had neither the time, money nor resources to determine the facts of native title.

Future exploration and development of lands previously classed as 'vacant crown land' would cease or proceed only with great uncertainty until there was a regime for the determination of native title. There had to be a register. Developers had to know with whom they needed to deal. Aborigines living in remote areas had no real desire to jump the hoops to have their names entered on a register. Had they sought legal advice, they would have been informed that their common law native title rights were recognised by the courts. Were a State government to act as if those rights did not exist, the common law native title holders would have been assured that their rights, though legally fragile before 1975, were now buttressed by the *RDA*. State governments wanting a comprehensive land registration system needed to lure native title holders into the tent of registration. State officials could use only a carrot because the Commonwealth's *RDA* precluded the use of the stick. There would be a need for some additional rights being offered native title holders in exchange for their subjecting themselves to the rigours of registration. There would also have to be an offer of some additional rights in exchange for Aboriginal agreement to a validation regime which rendered certain all dealings on native title land since 1975.

The main concern of the Aboriginal leadership was the relationship between them and mining companies. Justice Woodward in his 1974 Royal Commission report on Aboriginal land rights considered that 'Of all the questions I have had to consider, that of mineral rights has probably caused me the most difficulty and concern'. He concluded: 'I believe that to deny Aborigines the right to prevent mining on their land is to deny the reality of their land rights'. He reached this conclusion after setting out the mining industry's submissions in some detail, 'because while accepting many of the points made, I am unable to accept the main result contended for'. Despite the key Woodward recommendation on the control of mining, which is regularly invoked by Aboriginal leaders, Prime Minister Keating refused to grant a veto to native title holders. Instead he offered only a right to negotiate at the exploration and development stages. If after six months, native title holders did not reach agreement with the miner, there would be recourse to independent arbitration. Should the arbitral body agree with the Aboriginal demand that mining not proceed, the State minister would have power to override the decision.

Aboriginal leaders had long been mistrustful of the States and presumed that any Commonwealth government, no matter which party was in power, would be more respectful of Aboriginal rights than the States. The Aborigines conceded the need for a registration system but they wanted guaranteed access to a national tribunal which had the proper hallmarks of independence from industry and government and sensitivity to differing cultural aspirations. They also wanted an effective, resourced system of representative bodies which could assist and represent native title claimants in their dealings with government and developers. The Keating government was agreeable to these demands because anything less would have left Aborigines so dissatisfied with the proposed compromise that they would have stayed outside the registration tent, prepared to weather the demands of common law claims in the courts. Such action would have delayed interminably future developments on land.

Throughout 1993, most players assumed that only a small percentage of Aborigines would ever be able to establish a native title claim. Most indigenous Australians had been dispossessed of their traditional lands, either because they had been alienated to other persons prior to 1975, or because they had lost the necessary connection with the land. If, say, only five per cent of Aborigines could establish a claim, a just and proper settlement of the land issue called for the establishment of a land acquisition fund which would permit the dispossessed 95 per cent to purchase lands on the open market. The Keating government also agreed to a social justice package which would address other matters of disadvantage and marginalisation. The purpose of the *Native Title Act 1993 (NTA)* was to permit a return to certainty for business and government by means of a registration system and additional statutory rights acceptable to Aborigines so that all parties could own the outcome as fair, certain and workable.

Pastoralists still had nagging doubts about their entitlements and whether or not native title could exist on a pastoral lease. In the final stages of the negotiations for the *NTA* in 1993, the Aborigines, pastoralists and government did a deal. It was midnight and the miners were at home in bed. All parties had negotiated on the assumption that native title was extinguished on pastoral leases. The Aborigines won concessions. The *NTA* would not itself guarantee the extinguishment of native title on pastoral leases—the presumption would merely be stated in the preamble, and it would be up to the courts to decide the matter.

The only pastoral leases to be validated were the 11 thought to have been issued on vacant crown land since 1975. Being validated by legislation, those leases would extinguish native title, with provision for compensation of any native title holders. Meanwhile Aborigines would trade on the uncertainty about all other pastoral leases when it came to dealing with mining companies. The land acquisition fund could be used for the purchase of pastoral leases on the open market. The legislation would permit a revival of native title on pastoral leases once purchased. Pastoral leases in

Western Australia, the Northern Territory and South Australia had always permitted some ongoing Aboriginal access to the land for hunting, fishing, camping and ceremony. Those rights of access and use would continue.

The pastoralists won their concession. They would be able to continue their pastoral operations and renew their leases without having to negotiate with Aborigines. But the miners were left in the dark. Until the law was certain, they did not know if they would have to negotiate with local Aborigines before getting access to white pastoral properties. They would definitely have to negotiate in future with native title holders who purchased pastoral leases. Lawyers for the Keating government in later litigation submitted that native title was extinguished on pastoral leases.

As a result of this deal, the National Farmers Federation (NFF) understood that the Aborigines would drop their common law claims to native title on pastoral leases. They thought the *Wik* litigation over pastoral leases would be discontinued. Noel Pearson told the National Press Club on 18 November 1993: 'As to the question of whether native title survives with all forms of other title as a co-existent title, that is a matter that is unresolved by the High Court and may well be the subject of future litigation'. When interviewed after his address by Rural Press, he said:

> I rule out the possibility in Queensland of people pursuing any rights in relation to pastoral leases owned by non-Aboriginal people. I rule that out categorically, because there is a facility now available for us to purchase under the Land Fund, and to convert pastoral leases into native title.

While pastoralists thought the 1993 deal closed the door on any expansion of native title on pastoral leases, Aborigines thought the deal left the door slightly ajar for future court determinations.

Initially the Keating government had hoped to cut a legislative deal with the Coalition parties in Opposition. That proved impossible especially once Peter Reith took control of the Coalition agenda as Shadow Minister of State. He impugned the High Court for the *Mabo* decision and made it clear that the Coalition would not be party to any enhancement of common law native title rights by the addition of a statutory right to negotiate with mining companies. Prime Minister Keating then had no choice but to court the minor parties in the Senate, which were more pro-Aboriginal than his finely balanced Cabinet, which included strong pro-development ministers.

As Christmas approached in 1993, Paul Keating had to decide how many additional concessions he could make to the minor parties in the Senate which were seeking greater concessions for native title claimants. Each concession cost something in terms of certainty and workability for other stakeholders. The statutory right to negotiate with mining companies was worrying for the mining industry, which insisted on a strict threshold test for the registration of any claim before such a right would be exercisable.

The Keating government had wanted any application for registration to be accompanied by a declaration that the applicant, having conducted a search of all relevant land title registers, believed that native title had not been extinguished. The registrar was then to have the power to reject an application if of the opinion that native title had been extinguished. In particular, the registrar would be able to reject an application if she considered that it did not contain sufficient information about any physical connection that may be required by common law between the applicants, their descendants and the land. Aborigines were very disturbed by this physical connection test and the burdens being imposed on them before they could even lodge a claim.

Courtesy of the Western Australian Greens led by Christabel Chamarette, the entire threshold test was rewritten by the Senate. This was a high risk strategy by the Aboriginal groups and their supporters. If the threshold bar were set too low, there would be a spate of spurious claims as well as multiple conflicting claims over the same land areas. Keating had been forewarned of this difficulty. On the face of it, these amendments were more favourable to native title claimants. They were however to prove a future headache to land councils and other representative bodies especially in the Goldfields area of Western Australia where up to 17 claims were lodged over the one area.

Keating made the political judgment that the concessions on the threshold test had to be made if the legislation were to pass the Senate. The federal Coalition was so removed from the possibility of negotiated compromise that the Liberal Party would not agree to any amendments in the Senate even if they were supported by industry groups. National Party Senator Julian McGauran later described the 1993 native title debate as a painful one: 'Like World War I army commanders, the Liberals preferred a war of attrition fought from the trenches. Despite the urging of industry and senior Nationals, the Liberals would not shift their votes. They had stopped listening'. McGauran described the result: 'Security for pastoral leases was retained but the interests of the mining sector—which generates more than 50 per cent of Australia's merchandise export income—were cast off'.

Aborigines were fortified that they now had access to the courts and influence in the Senate. Never before had indigenous Australia had such a strong bargaining position with the government of the day. Unfortunately some of the Senate changes obtained by the Aborigines were to create future problems. The miners felt excluded by government and snubbed by the Senate. They were convinced that the combination of Keating's right to negotiate with the Senate's low threshold test would render the legislation unworkable.

3 | THE UNRESOLVED ISSUES WITH THE *NATIVE TITLE ACT 1993*

When the National Native Title Tribunal (NNTT) opened its doors for business in 1994, there was a flood of native title applications. The 1993 Senate threshold test simply required the applicant to state the belief that native title had not been extinguished. The registrar then had no option but to accept the claim for registration unless of the opinion that the claim was frivolous or vexatious or a *prima facie* case could not be made for it. The matter would then be referred to a presidential member of the tribunal who would give the applicant an opportunity to be heard before deciding whether the claim could be accepted. A 1995 Federal Court decision gave the registrar no option but to accept all claims for registration other than those which were frivolous or vexatious. The floodgates were open and attention was on developments in the Gulf of Carpentaria.

In September 1990, CRA had announced the Century Zinc discovery, forecasting the world's largest zinc mine. In 1993, Pasminco, an Australian company, took over full ownership of the Budel zinc smelter in Holland. The Dutch government insisted that the smelter reduce its pollution levels or close by June 1998. Pasminco was hopeful it could use the pure zinc from Century. If the project were to proceed, the miners would have to deal with various Aboriginal groups, including those claiming native title over the two square kilometre mine site, those claiming an interest along the 300 kilometre pipeline route and the community on Mornington Island 150 kilometres out to sea, who had environmental concerns. Much of the land along the pipeline route was subject to pastoral lease. The outstanding legal question was: could native title exist on a Queensland pastoral lease or was native title necessarily extinguished by the grant of the lease?

Queensland pastoral leases differed from the equivalent leases in Western Australia, the Northern Territory and South Australia in that they did not contain any written reservation for continued Aboriginal access to the land. In May 1994, the NNTT indicated that it would not accept claims over pastoral leases which did not contain reservations in favour of Aborigines. The North Ganalanja Aboriginal Corporation, the representative body for some of the Aborigines interested in the Century project, challenged this decision in the courts. The Aborigines lost all the way until they got to the High Court. The High Court decision was not delivered until almost two years after the controversy first arose before the NNTT. Meanwhile the miners had asked the Goss Labor government to issue the notices to all affected parties, thereby triggering the right to negotiate under the *NTA*. The Queensland government declined on the basis of their legal advice that a Queensland pastoral lease extinguished native title. When the High Court delivered its judgment a fortnight after the election of the Howard government, all parties were put on notice by the court that claims to native title on pastoral leases were 'fairly arguable'. Until then, the Queensland government had acted in good faith. Presuming that native title did not exist on pastoral leases, the government had continued granting interests over pastoral lease land without following the procedures of the *NTA*. From March 1996, it was a different matter.

All companies in the Century project had to deal with a complex political cocktail—new legislation, a change of government in Brisbane followed by a new government in Canberra in March 1996, and new findings by the courts favouring Aboriginal claimants who had not yet proved native title. Under the leadership of Leon Davis, CRA (the parent company of Century Zinc) had announced in early 1995 that it accepted the central tenets of the *NTA* and that it was committed to engaging with Aborigines living in mining areas to find mutually advantageous outcomes. CRA did not want to get bogged down in legalistic arguments about the extinguishment of native title on pastoral leases. It was happy to talk and negotiate with all local Aboriginal groups.

CRA and the Commonwealth engaged or provided funds for the nation's leading practitioners of Aboriginal and industry negotiation. These included Tracker Tilmouth from the Central Land Council, Hal Wootten QC who had been a very sympathetic member of the Royal Commission into Aboriginal Deaths in Custody, Ron Castan QC who had argued the *Mabo* case for the native title claimants and Warren Snowden, the ex-ALP Member for the

Northern Territory and ex-staffer from the Central Land Council. From late 1994, Aborigines throughout the Gulf region were consulted. A broad coalition of Aboriginal interests ultimately recorded a 12–11 vote approving the project and the CRA offer, which included the transfer of pastoral leases and three million dollars a year over the 20 year life of the mine.

For any major project of this sort, the company required absolute certainty of title. CRA thought this would be best achieved by the Queensland government compulsorily acquiring the mine site and the pipeline corridor. Both governments and all major political parties agreed that if the project enjoyed broad support from the local Aboriginal communities, it should go ahead in the national interest.

Under the *NTA*, a State government cannot compulsorily acquire land until it has first sought agreement with the company and Aboriginal native title claimants under the right to negotiate regime. Ultimately, government can give a project the go-ahead, but only after all parties have negotiated for six months. If agreement is not reached, an independent tribunal can then give a determination. The State or Commonwealth minister has the power to overrule the tribunal and authorise a mining lease or compulsory acquisition of land in the national interest. Unless agreement is reached, the entire process could take up to 14 months.

There had been Aboriginal native title claimants on the books and known to have the right to negotiate over Century since February 1996. The Queensland government did not initiate the right to negotiate through the issue of notices until late May 1996. Within a month, Premier Borbidge made it clear that he had no intention of negotiating with the likes of Murrandoo Yanner, Co-ordinator of the Carpentaria Land Council. Yanner's father was a well respected Aboriginal leader in the Gulf region. Yanner is a charismatic, tertiary educated man with training in the media. He used colourful language against the government and the company, claiming they 'wanted to steamroll us with a bulldozer'. Borbidge thought the company had negotiated for long enough. He overlooked the *NTA*'s requirement that the government negotiate in good faith with the company and the Aboriginal claimants. Government could not just sit on the sidelines waiting for the negotiation period to expire.

Premier Borbidge wanted to legislate the exclusion of the Aboriginal right to negotiate with government, explaining that the compulsory acquisition would have 'minute' impact on any native title. Borbidge could not do this without complementary Commonwealth legislation. But he was handing Prime Minister Howard a poisoned chalice. The Commonwealth always had power to exclude a proposed compulsory acquisition of land from the right to negotiate if the minister 'considers the act will have minimal effect on any native title concerned'. Warwick Parer, the Minister for Resources and Energy, had not done so. He could not do so in good faith. If there were only minimal impact on native title, the minister was required to be satisfied only that the native title holders would be appropriately consulted about access to the land. Introducing the legislation in 1993, Keating had told Parliament: 'Classes of grant can be excluded from the negotiation process altogether where they would have minimal impact on native title. Certain prospecting and exploration permits would be likely to fall within this category'. The Queensland government took the view that temporary interference with the land only for the purpose of laying a pipeline should have triggered the exemption in accordance with Keating's original intent. Government lawyers thought the exemption provision was unworkable because it would be challenged in the courts by disaffected native title claimants. This would then mean that despite the original intention of the Keating government, a full blown right to negotiate would be exercisable by native title claimants in all circumstances.

Meanwhile Murrandoo Yanner's strong opposition to the pipeline was gaining momentum among the Gulf Aborigines, who were feeling locked out from the discussions in Brisbane and Canberra. CRA realised it was time to get back to the bush, demonstrate good faith and negotiate as the law required. Century Zinc became a test case rather than the exception to the *NTA*. Premier Borbidge was furious with the company for abandoning its call for special legislation to cover the project. The company decided to work within the constraints of the *NTA*. Moderate Aboriginal leaders on the national scene had been called in. Lois O'Donoghue maintained that a meeting of local Aborigines to determine the future of the project was properly constituted, and she stood by their 12–11 vote in favour of the mine. She said,

'ATSIC's role in the attempted resolution of differences over the proposed Century Zinc mine is to maintain a view of the broader, national implications of the handling of the dispute'. Some of the young, local Aboriginal leaders were distinctly unimpressed. Murrandoo Yanner, claiming a 22–0 vote against the mine by native title claimants, retorted: 'I have inside information that there is a deal going on between the top-level so-called Aboriginal leaders in this country, the State and Federal Government and CRA'. He called on Lois O'Donoghue to resign as ATSIC Chairperson 'before we are forced to drag her through the courts for having a direct pecuniary interest in the Century Mine'. She had no such interest.

At the end of the six month negotiation period, no agreement was reached and the matter was referred to arbitration. The Borbidge government appointed Bill Hayden as chief negotiator. In March 1997 Hayden published an explosive letter which he had sent to Borbidge. Having been federal leader of the ALP and then governor-general, Hayden knew his assessment of the workability of the *NTA* would impact strongly on the political debate. He described the right-to-negotiate process as 'haggling over the size of pots of money for different things' which encouraged excessive ambit claims to be made and rigidly pursued. He said:

> What became abundantly clear to me quite early is how complex, even confusing, the drafting of the relevant legislation is; the opportunities the legislation offers for outside manipulation of processes and for the adoption of measures which come perilously close at times to being extortion; the absence of any definition of who can be a claimant and the seemingly unlimited opportunities for people to register as such; the unrepresentativeness of some who register as claimants; the confusion and tensions which can become rampant as long-standing factional and family disputes within a tribal group manifest themselves at the expense of the issue to be settled; the jealousy and mistrust which can arise between different tribal bodies which can impair negotiating processes.

After the venting of Hayden's frustrations, the parties did reach agreement in May 1997, avoiding the need for formal arbitration. But the delays had been very costly for the company which had to honour its arrangements in the Netherlands. The whole process had angered the Borbidge government, which became convinced that the legal machinery for consultation and negotiation between native title claimants and miners should be trimmed as far as possible. Once amendments to the *NTA* were being debated in Parliament, Hayden's observations were sure to do harm to Aboriginal claims that the procedures of the *NTA* were workable. This saga highlighted a major problem of workability of the Act which was playing itself out all over the country.

Meanwhile the work of the NNTT had been sharply curtailed by the High Court's *Brandy* decision in February 1995, which stopped federal tribunals from being able to exercise judicial power. For years, the Commonwealth Parliament had been granting dispute resolution functions to bodies which were not courts—bodies such as the Human Rights and Equal Opportunity Commission. The *Brandy* decision threw an enormous spoke in this wheel of cheaper, less formal Commonwealth dispute resolution. A determination of rights between conflicting parties could now be made at a federal level only by a properly constituted court exercising judicial power. Any disagreement about the existence of native title would have to be resolved by the Federal Court and not by the NNTT.

In 1993, the Aborigines had come away with two significant wins in the negotiation of the *NTA* —the right to negotiate and guaranteed access to a national tribunal. The right to negotiate was under pressure, with big projects such as Century being bogged down, and with an increasing number of conflicting claims, especially in the Western Goldfields. Guaranteed access to a national tribunal was now under threat, given that any federal dispute would have to go through the more formal and expensive processes of the Federal Court. In the light of the High Court's 1996 observation that native title co-existing on State pastoral leases was 'fairly arguable', there would be pressure from the States for State tribunals, rather than the Federal Court having to determine the relationship between native title and rights of pastoralists with State titles. Regardless of any change of government in Canberra, there was sure to be pressure on the two major gains made by Aborigines, in part because these two gains were proving more cumbersome to other parties than originally predicted and promised by the Keating government in 1993. The problems were exacerbated by the abysmally low threshold test designed by the Greens.

In late 1995, the Keating government introduced its own legislation to address the problems raised by the High Court in the *Brandy* case and by the complexities of the Century negotiations. While retaining guaranteed Aboriginal access to the Federal Court for the determination of a native title claim, the Keating government accepted the need to raise the bar on the threshold test. Under the new Keating test, the registrar would have been able to have regard to whatever information was considered appropriate in addition to the application, before deciding whether there was a *prima facie* case for the claim. There would have been an appeal to the Federal Court if the Registrar refused to register a claim.

Due to the dissolution of the House of Representatives and the following election campaign, the Keating amendments never saw the light of day. The problems with the threshold test were increased by the High Court's interpretation of it in the *Waanyi* case which related to the native title applications in the Century Zinc area. The court gave judgment a fortnight after the election of the Howard government, accepting the rationale of the 1993 Senate amendments as being the need for negotiation and agreement rather than judicial determination of complex issues. The court thought the legislation was designed to enhance the prospect of an amicable relationship between neighbouring occupiers. The judges were anxious to avoid a situation whereby the application for registration,

> which was intended to lead to the formation of a preliminary opinion would become—as happened in the present case—a contest between parties with opposing interests and the controversy would be settled not by agreement between 'parties' or by decision of the Federal Court as the Act intends but by a presidential member acting administratively.

During the 1996 federal election, the Cape York Land Council pulled a rabbit out of the hat and announced the heads of agreement for the Cape York Land Agreement. The message was: 'Negotiation at the regional level can work. There is no need for national legislation which interferes with the prospect of such agreement'. Parties to the agreement were Aborigines, environmentalists and local pastoralists represented by the Cattlemen's Union. The NFF smelt a rat. So did the miners, who viewed the agreement as a 'black-green' sweetheart arrangement which would be a disincentive for new mining activity in the Cape. National Party Premier Rob Borbidge was adamant that the agreement be scuttled. It was. Once John Howard became Prime Minister there was no place for such an agreement. There was bound to be comprehensive amendment to the 1993 legislation, restricting the right to negotiate, raising the bar of the threshold test, and granting States the right to set up their own processes for determining native title.

While the Western Australian Goldfields were being claimed and counterclaimed, and as the Century machinations were attracting national headlines, an ambit claim by the Yorta Yorta people of Victoria was dragging on. It went first through the mediation process, which commenced with the acceptance of the claim by the NNTT in May 1994, and then through full blown Federal Court proceedings, which commenced in May 1995. Three years later, the court had heard evidence for 100 days. There are 278 claimants representing 4500 community members who claim that their traditional country spans the Murray, Ovens, Goulburn and Edward Rivers. Their QC, Bryan Keon-Cohen, who appeared in the *Mabo* case, drafted a claim using the words of the High Court order in *Mabo*. The Aborigines are claiming 'rights of possession, occupation, use and enjoyment to all of the claimed area to the exclusion of all others'. The claimed area includes the Barmah State Forest. The claim covers anything up to 4000 square kilometres as well as compensation for extinguishment of title to another 16,000 square kilometres. There are over 500 respondents who claim that their various titles and permits from the Crown would be adversely affected by the recognition of any claim to exclusive use and occupation. Much to the consternation of local farmers, shire councils and the two State governments either side of the Murray, the applicants claim:

> all water which, from time to time, may be found within the claimed areas, whether such waters are, at any time, stationary or flowing, or located in nat-

> ural or man made water courses or dams. Such claims extend to the banks and beds, underlying or supporting such waters, and all natural resources found therein.

In 1997–98, the case cost ATSIC $865,000. The case is sure to be appealed. The Yorta Yorta claim to exclusive possession and use of the land to the exclusion of all others became a model precedent for many other claims. Farmers receiving such claims in the mail were horrified, failing to see how the language was in any way suggestive of co-existing rights. They saw such claims as demands for their own dispossession.

No matter which party was in power at the national level, the Yorta Yorta litigation created a demand not only for a stricter threshold test, but also for legislative certainty about water rights, the entitlements of shire councils wanting to deliver services and a definition of which titles granted a right of exclusive possession, thereby extinguishing native title prior to 1975. By early 1996, there was a long ledger of demands for amendment to the *NTA* in the name of workability, certainty and reasonableness. Century Zinc, the overlapping mosaic of claims in the Western Australian Goldfields, and the Yorta Yorta claim were the big number items indicating underlying difficulties with the operation of the *NTA*.

4 | THE NEW DIRECTION OF THE HOWARD GOVERNMENT 1996

The election of the Howard government on 2 March 1996 provided new challenges for the moderate Aboriginal leaders who believed in negotiation and reconciliation. At his first prime ministerial press conference, John Howard said that any changes to the *NTA* would be made in a way 'that doesn't violate the principles of the *Racial Discrimination Act*'. Noel Pearson, one of the key negotiators of the 1993 settlement, had said at the end of that process:

> For a long time, the only political currency which Aboriginal people could use was their refusal to be involved. Now that the non-Aboriginal legal system has offered something in the way of rights, however narrow, to refuse to play the game and to fail to appreciate its rules and limitations, no longer seems smart.

The Coalition parties had been out of government for 13 years. They had opposed the setting up of ATSIC. They had opposed the *NTA*. Nick Minchin, appointed to oversee the Howard government's approach to native title, had been negative in his slight contribution to the 1993 debate.

In the initial months of his prime ministership, John Howard went to great lengths to distinguish the High Court's *Mabo* decision from the Keating government's native title legislation. Of *Mabo* he oft repeated: 'The substance of that decision, now with the passage of time, seems completely unexceptionable to me. It appears to have been based on a great deal of logic and fairness and proper principle'. Howard's concern was with 'the unwarranted extensions of it engaged in by the former Labor government'. The rules of engagement were changing again.

In its first month in office, the Howard government received a detailed submission from the Minerals Council of Australia (MCA) seeking a comprehensive overhaul of the *NTA*. The Howard government announced its intention to take away the right to negotiate with mining companies at the exploration phase.

Richard Court, Premier of Western Australia, was even pressing for the abolition of the right to negotiate at all stages, claiming:

> Excluding exploration from the right to negotiate only creates greater uncertainty at the mining stage and many companies will not spend large amounts on exploration if there is doubt about their ability to develop resources that may be found.

Three months after the election of the Howard government, Minchin introduced amendments to the Keating legislation 'confident that anyone who is prepared to approach this Bill in a fair-minded way will conclude that it does not alter the basic philosophy of the *Native Title Act*'. This was a big ask given Minchin's hostility to the original Act, which he had labelled 'bad law' in the 1993 parliamentary debate, claiming it created inherently racist title, while dangerously and profoundly undermining the sovereignty of the States. Minchin had a strong public commitment to passing land management back to the States and winding back additional statutory rights granted to native title holders by the Commonwealth Parliament.

Even before the *Wik* decision, the Howard government proposed extensive amendment to the *NTA*. In May 1996, they published a discussion paper with the neutral title *Towards a More Workable Native Title Act*. Many of the proposed amendments were necessary in the interests of workability, with the benefit of experience and in the light of recent High Court decisions. These amendments would have been sponsored by any government no matter which party was in power. The devil was in the detail, with some amendments in the name of workability being a cloak for ideological stripping away of Aboriginal rights.

Prior to the *Wik* decision it was not known whether native title could survive on a pastoral lease. Even if it did, it did not affect mortgagability nor renewal of leases. Under the Keating legislation, a pastoral lease could automatically be renewed without the need to negotiate with native title holders provided the lease contained identical terms, conditions and reservations for the protection of Aboriginal access. The Howard government wanted to allow a pastoralist to renew a lease for longer terms than the original lease, and to vary terms of the lease, permitting the pastoralist to engage in non-pastoral activities. If native title were affected by the extension of lease terms or conditions or by 'permissible pastoral lease related acts', the native title holder would be entitled only to compensation. Should these additional rights interfere with native title rights, government, and not the pastoralist, would pay for any reduction in the native title rights.

The NFF had claimed that uncertainty about native title was causing problems for pastoralists seeking assistance from the banks. This was a real furphy as revealed by Ian Gilbert, Director (Legal) with the Australian Bankers Association, who told a national meeting of Aborigines, miners and pastoralists on 2 June 1996 that 'banks have been unable to identify instances or circumstances in which native title rights and the exercise of them would come into conflict with the bank's interests as a security holder'. Gilbert said:

> I have canvassed a number of member banks very carefully over recent days about the issues raised in Senator Minchin's paper and the issue of native title generally and, without exception, I have been unable to turn up any incidents, from any member with whom I have spoken, of a concern over native title as an issue in so far as a bank and its lending and security position is concerned.

The miners who wanted to restrict the application of the right to negotiate found a listening ear in the new government. Over 40 per cent of the Australian land mass is under pastoral lease. Miners would prefer to deal only with the pastoralists, if necessary buying them out. The *Wik* case was yet to determine if the miners would also have to deal with Aborigines who had maintained connections with these lands. The miners wanted a political guarantee and legislative certainty rather than waiting for a High Court test case. They quietly set about convincing government to bring in a stricter threshold test for registering claims and to restrict the right to negotiate so that Aborigines would not have two bites of the cherry, at both the exploration and the development stages.

In June 1996, the High Court commenced the hearing of argument in the *Wik* proceedings. Two different Aboriginal groups, the Wik and the Thayorre had conflicting claims to the same area of land. The queen's counsel appearing for the pastoralists claimed that pastoralists' titles were being disturbed by uncertainty over the renewal and mortgagability of leases. Questioned by the bench, counsel had to admit that the *NTA* guaranteed renewal of leases on identical terms and conditions to the existing leases. He limply claimed that native title could be a concern to a mortgagee, 'perhaps not strictly a legal effect but disturbance of the title'. This assertion could not be reconciled with the earlier public statements of the Australian Bankers Association.

While the pastoralists were out front in the public debate, claiming uncertainty on all sides, the miners took a different approach. In 1993, the mining industry charge against the Keating government had been led by strident spokesmen such as Hugh Morgan. This time around the industry needed to adopt a different policy. The industry leaders knew they had the Coalition parties on board, being part of their natural constituency. Any winding back of the right to negotiate would be approved by the Senate only with the support of the ALP or of the minor parties and independents. The Democrats and Greens were unlikely to support such a move. The industry set about wooing the ALP opposition about the unworkability of a right to negotiate, both at the exploration and development stages. They were careful not to offend Aboriginal leaders lest they alienate Senator Harradine, who held the balance of power in the Senate.

Australia's most senior mining executive, Leon Davis, Chief Operating Officer of RTZ-CRA (now known as Rio Tinto), addressing the Australian Business in Europe Group in August 1996, said:

> Our experience of negotiating with Aboriginal communities has taught us that Aboriginal leaders face a herculean task. I understand this difficulty. It is the greatest challenge facing the current generation of Aboriginal leaders. So I urge more acknowledgment of the efforts of those Aboriginal leaders representing the spirit of reconciliation and an understanding of the pressures upon them.

In its formal presentation to the national conference marking the twentieth anniversary of the Commonwealth Parliament's land rights legislation, CRA, through its Vice President Paul Wand, expressed regret to Aboriginal Australians on a number of counts: for the failure to prevent the destruction of Aboriginal housing at Mapoon, Cape York, when bauxite mining commenced; for having ignored traditional owners whose lands were mined in the Pilbara; and for the scars on the land and the scars on the spirit of the people at the Argyle diamond mine in the Kimberley.

At the same conference, Gough Whitlam told Aboriginal Australia how he had approached his commission to put the case for the Sydney Olympics to African nations. He had told the world of our robust record on indigenous rights and our claim to be second to none in the international protection of human rights. He was putting the nation on notice that if the government dropped the bar on either, we would have won the Games on false pretences and would be making a rod for our own backs in the international community in the lead-up to 2000. Three days later, as if to illustrate Whitlam's point, there was a large Aboriginal protest rally outside Parliament House. Though much more peaceful than the earlier unionists' march which stormed through the doors of Parliament House, it culminated in a ritual burning of the Australian flag by Murrandoo Yanner and his supporters.

The Century Zinc question had not been resolved by negotiation within the time limit set down in the *NTA*, and there was an increasing backlog in claims registered in Western Australia. There were problems with infrastructure developments such as pipelines which, though causing only temporary disruption to the enjoyment of native title rights, were causing enormous headaches for developers who had to deal with conflicting claimants along narrow corridors of land hundreds of kilometres long. The focus was once again on Queensland, particularly on the Teneco pipeline in the southwest of the state, which was to run from the Cooper Basin to Wallumbilla. In the end the State government and the developer, who was anxious to proceed, decided to engage the services of both the Bidjara and Gunggari groups to clear the last section of the route. Further west on the pipeline route there was a long running dispute between well known local Aboriginal identity Hazel McKellar and the newly constituted Goolburri Land Council. She had walked part of the route, which she knew well from 30 years of continued contact. But the representative body dispensed with her services. Her description of local Aboriginal antipathies is symptomatic of the problems wherever development is proposed across uncertain native title boundaries. In 1997, she addressed a conference on 'The Structure and Experience of

Racism in Australia' and reflected on what native title has brought:

> The conflict in the community organisations and neighbouring towns as they struggle for power was unreal when native title came on the scene.
>
> I was forbidden to walk this area as it was claimed I was a non-traditional person. However, there was no mention of any Bunthamaka representatives on the Land Council.
>
> When you talk about discrimination practised by white people, well, it comes from our own black people too, and I did a lot for those people, I believe, anyway, and all I got from the younger people was abuse: 'How dare you go out there, walking our country'. I said, 'Well, where were you twenty years ago? Would you know where your grandfather's grave is at South Comongin? Would you know where so and so is buried in Gininburra? Would you know whether the campsite was at Nockaboorara Waterhole or Barulyah, where there were massacres, where they were shot, where you walk around the sand dunes and see the bullets lying there?'
>
> This has hurt and frustrated me very much, and so I have been off the scene for a few years. This is what is happening, because when they put me and my son off, the fellow they put on to walk the area was a non-traditional person too, but he was flavour of the month.

Government and industry were becoming convinced that the right to negotiate in these cases was simply an opportunity for duplicating financial reward. They had renewed determination to wind back the right to negotiate. The Howard government issued an 'Exposure Draft' of amendments to the right to negotiate in October 1996, two months before the High Court's decision on *Wik*. It is important to appreciate that most of the Ten Point Plan, which was to emerge in the following May after the *Wik* decision, was not a response to the *Wik* decision. It was government policy formulated by industry before the election of the Howard government and refined by the government during its first year in office. It was policy to be legislated regardless of which way the *Wik* decision went.

Whatever the High Court would eventually decide about the co-existence of native title and pastoral leases, the Commonwealth and State governments were intent on permitting pastoralists to diversify their primary production activities. They wanted to do this whether or not the leases contained terms guaranteeing continued Aboriginal access and use. The Commonwealth government was insistent that a State government be able to extend the terms and conditions of pastoral leases no matter what the High Court might say. Whether or not there was co-existing native title on pastoral leases, government was adamant that it would not trigger the right to negotiate with mining companies. The native title holders would have the same procedural rights as the pastoralist, which usually amounted only to an entitlement to compensation for actual disturbance to the land. All other native title holders would be restricted to a once-only right to negotiate which could be suspended by the State government in the public interest. None of these policy positions was a response to *Wik*. They were set in stone by the Howard government before the *Wik* decision.

The Commonwealth government's strategy was: distinguish *Mabo* from the statutory accretions added by the Keating government; shame the ALP into admitting the unworkability of its 1993 legislation; convince the Senate of the political stupidity of holding up further development in the name of protecting native title; scrape away the accretions in the name of certainty and workability; and limit any effect that the High Court's judgment on *Wik* might have. The government always claimed to be acting in a non-discriminatory way, to be concerned only with taking away special rights which had been given to native title holders by Parliament and which were holding up development costing the country jobs and security.

The Howard government was committed to responding to the concerns of industry and State governments. Facing charges of discrimination and weakness in the face of Pauline Hanson's growth in popularity, the government was happy to sponsor a bipartisan resolution in the Parliament on 30 October 1996, reaffirming 'its commitment to the right of all Australians to enjoy equal rights and be treated with equal respect regardless of race, colour, creed or origin', and reaffirming 'its commitment to the process of reconciliation with Aboriginal and Torres Strait Islander people, in the context of redressing their profound social and economic disadvantage'.

The Prime Minister said, 'It is in the national interest to send a clear and unambiguous signal, particularly to the nations of our region, of the kind of society we are'. A month later during the Western Australian election campaign, Deputy Prime Minister Tim Fischer attacked the High Court for its delay in delivering a decision on *Wik*. He told miners and pastoralists in Kalgoorlie, 'I am frustrated and angered by the delay in handing down of the decision by the High Court'. He believed the delay was 'a legitimate matter for public consideration and I state my concerns on behalf of thousands of pastoralists in remote and regional Australia'. The Chief Justice took strong exception to the Deputy Prime Minister's attack, reminding him that public confidence in the constitutional institutions of Government was critical to the stability of society:

> By a convention which is based in sound practice, judges do not (and certainly should not) publicly attack the members of the political branches of government, and the members of the political branches of government do not (and certainly should not) attack the judges except on a substantive motion in the Parliament.

Mr Fischer pleaded that his remarks were made 'against the background of incorrect advice' he had received. No matter what the High Court decided on *Wik*, the Howard government had already set its course to wind back any additional statutory rights granted to native title holders and to withdraw the Commonwealth as far as possible from land management in the States. The High Court decision would ultimately require some fine tuning of the policy parameters. It would also provide government with another demon to slay in the name of workability, certainty and the national interest.

5 | THE *WIK* COCKTAIL 1996

After *Mabo*, most lawyers (I included) thought it would be very difficult for Aborigines to establish the co-existence of native title on pastoral leases. For example, this exchange occurred between myself and Senator Chris Ellison, Chair of the Parliamentary Joint Committee on Native Title and the Aboriginal and Torres Strait Islander Land Fund, at a hearing in Darwin on 28 August 1996:

> *Chair*: Reading between the lines, you are anticipating that the High Court will come down in favour of saying that pastoral leases do not extinguish native title rights.
>
> *Father Brennan*: No; I am not anticipating that. The only thing that I have written or said publicly on this was probably prior to reading the transcript of the oral argument, where it seemed to me that in terms of logic it was going to be very difficult for the Aborigines to have a win, and that what was essential was to maintain what was called in the *Mabo* judgment the 'skeleton of principle'. It seemed to me on my reading of *Mabo* that basically it was only the Crown that could extinguish native title, and the question of whether native title had been extinguished is always a question of law or fact. If it is a question of a Crown grant, it is a question of law, and you look at the grant to see whether or not there has been a power to exclude the traditional native title holders. If it be not a Crown grant but a Crown use, then it is probably a mixed question of law and fact as to whether there has been that extinction.
>
> It seems to me that, in terms of strict logic, the problem that has confronted the advocates for Aborigines in the *Wik* case has been this: even in the most liberal reservations in the pastoral leases, such as in South Australia, there is the capacity for Aborigines to be excluded, for example, from regions 200 or 500 metres from bores or houses or whatever. What happens is that the only thing the Crown ever does is to grant the lease. The leaseholder later builds a house or a bore. By virtue of having built the house or bore, the leaseholder has for all time excluded Aborigines from access to that land. Given that native title can only be extinguished by the Crown and not by a third party, what did the Crown ever do? All the Crown ever did was to grant the lease in

the first instance. That is the conceptual problem which has confronted the Aboriginal groups in relation to the *Wik* case.

We see in the oral argument in the transcript that basically some of the High Court justices—particularly Justice McHugh—are, it seems to me, wrestling with the question of whether a pastoral lease is truly a lease and whether all pastoral leases can be properly categorised in this way. So it is some of those ambiguities which may give a window of opportunity to Aboriginal groups, but there will have to be not only that window of opportunity but something in terms of the 'skeleton of principle' whereby there can be certainty.

Chair: Thank you.

Father Brennan: Needless to say, I hope I am wrong.

I was wrong. Just as the country was closing down for Christmas drinks in 1996, the High Court handed down the decision in *The Wik Peoples* v *Queensland*. All judges upheld the validity of the bauxite mining leases granted in 1957. The court was unanimous in dispensing with arguments about a fiduciary duty which could threaten the validity of Crown grants before 1975. Three judges put it very starkly. They could not accept that a fiduciary duty 'can be owed by the Crown to the holders of native title in the exercise of a statutory power to alienate land whereby their native title in or over that land is liable to be extinguished without their consent and contrary to their interests'.

The co-existence of native title on pastoral leases was another matter. The court had to consider two pastoral holdings. The Mitchellton Pastoral Holding of 535 square miles was subject to a 30 year lease for pastoral purposes only which was issued in 1915. The lessees never took possession and the lease was forfeited in 1918 for non-payment of rent. Another lease was issued in 1919 and surrendered two years later, after which the land was set aside as a reserve for Aborigines. The Holroyd River Holding of 1119 square miles was subject to a 30 year lease issued in 1945 for pastoral purposes only. A new lease was granted in 1975. It was not restricted to pastoral purposes only, but it was subject to development conditions requiring the lessees to improve some of the land, sow a seed production area, fence the holding and maintain all improvements.

Court watchers always expected the *Wik* decision to be a close call. By a narrow majority of four–three, the court decided that a pastoral lease does not necessarily confer rights of exclusive possession on the pastoralist. Of the 1992 bench which decided *Mabo*, two had retired. In *Mabo*, Chief Justice Mason was one of the four justices who thought native title had been extinguished on the land subject to the sardine factory lease. Justice Deane was one of the three judges who presumably thought native title continued to exist despite the grant of the lease. Justices Mason and Deane had been replaced by Justices Gummow and Kirby. Court watchers always expected that Justice Kirby would favour the continued co-existence of native title on pastoral leases. They expected that Justice Gummow would have followed the reasoning of those justices who found native title extinguished by the grant of a lease. To the advantage of native title claimants, he did not. So the decision went four–three the other way. Daryl Melham, the enthusiastic Shadow Minister for Aboriginal Affairs, later commented that the four–three *Wik* decision reconfirmed his belief in God. Gareth Evans responded, 'But you didn't know his name was Gummow'.

The four judges in the *Wik* majority all wrote separate judgments. These four disagreed among themselves on some key issues. The minority of three judges put their name to one judgment written by Chief Justice Brennan who had written the lead judgment in *Mabo*. It was going to be difficult to argue that *Wik* was simply a logical extension of *Mabo*.

All judges were agreed that the rights and obligations of the pastoralist depended on the terms of the lease and the law under which it was granted. The minority thought a pastoral lease was a lease in the common law sense. It conferred a right of exclusive possession subject to any rights of access allowed to third parties by the lease or the statute. The majority thought the mere grant of a pastoral lease does not necessarily extinguish any remaining native title rights. The majority viewed a pastoral lease as a unique Australian statutory creation. No guidance was to be obtained by looking at the general law of leases. The majority conceded that there could be some conflict between the rights of a pastoral lessee and the ongoing rights of native title holders. If there were no conflict of rights, the rights of each could co-exist. If there were a conflict, the native title holders would come off second best.

Aborigines and their supporters immediately assured the public that there was nothing to fear in the judgment because in the event of a conflict of rights, the rights of the pastoralist would always prevail and the rights of the native title holder would yield. But there were two problems for developers which could not be resolved by these words of assurance. Even if the surviving native title on a pastoral lease were simply the right to come once a year to hunt for kangaroo, that common law right would attract the 1993 right to negotiate with a mining company, both at the exploration phase and at the mining phase. And though the four members of the majority spoke about prevailing pastoralists' rights, the concept of common law rights yielding to prevailing rights under a State title did not sit happily with the *RDA* and the shorthand test for non-discrimination that had been adopted in the past. The presumption had been that if you treated the native title holder in the same way as a freeholder, you would not be acting in a racially discriminatory way. A pastoralist wanting to build a dam on his pastoral lease knew that the dam once filled would be on land where native title had been extinguished. A dam could not be built on someone else's freehold without their consent. The building of the dam may have been simply a case of prevailing rights being asserted and yielding rights being extinguished. But it may have been an instance of an invalid action which offended the *RDA* or a future action, which under the terms of the *NTA* would require the agreement of the registered native title claimants if it were to be valid.

Many pastoral leases contain development conditions. If the pastoralist does not develop the land sufficiently, he is liable to forfeiture of the lease. Consider a simple case. A pastoralist has a lease with a development condition requiring him to erect a residence within five years. Let's say very hypothetically, it even specifies the area (half a hectare) and the location (by the creek). The issue of the lease does not extinguish native title over that half hectare. When the house is built, the native title holder will have a reduced bundle of rights and the pastoralist will have an increased bundle of rights if the development is lawful. The development condition is attached to a State lease granted pursuant to a State law which is subject to the *RDA*. The native title holder's bundle of rights has to be accorded the same Commonwealth protection as the pastoralist's bundle of rights. Under the *RDA*, native title holders enjoy their bundle of rights 'to the same extent' as any other titleholders.

Two members of the *Wik* majority, Justices Gaudron and Gummow, made it clear that it is not the grant of the lease with development conditions which trims back the native title rights. It is the performance of the act, the building of the house. To say there is no problem is to argue that the *RDA* has no application to this issue. That is, that the pastoralist can proceed and the native titleholder can be left unconsulted and uncompensated as if the *RDA* were not on the books.

The *Wik* minority judges raised a number of problems with the majority's hypothesis about the continuance and suspension of native title on pastoral leases. The minority said:

> Third party rights inconsistent with native title can be created by or with the authority of the legislature in exercise of legislative power but, as the power of State and Territory legislatures is now confined by the *Racial Discrimination Act*, a State or Territory law made or executive act done since that Act came into force cannot effect an extinguishment of native title if the law or executive act would not effect the extinguishment of a title acquired otherwise than as native title.

This view of the minority was supported by the majority judgment in the High Court's 1995 *Native Title Act* case when the judges said the *RDA*:

> ensures that Aborigines who are the holders of native title have the same security of enjoyment of their traditional rights over or in respect of land as others who are holders of title granted by the Crown and that a State law which purports to diminish that security of enjoyment is inoperative.

On that occasion, six of the seven High Court justices went on to say that the *RDA*:

> is superimposed on the common law and enhances the enjoyment of those human rights which affect native title so that Aboriginal holders are secure in the possession and enjoyment of native title to the same extent as the holders of other forms of title are secure in the possession and enjoyment of those titles.

A development act by a pastoralist committed since the *RDA* came into force cannot effect an impairment or extinguishment of native title if it could not validly effect the impairment or extinguishment of any other form of title. If native title is extinguished on developed land, the title must have been extinguished by a pre-1975 grant or by a development act approved by the grant, the development act having occurred before the passage of the *RDA*.

Given that pastoral leases are granted subject to State law, which since 1975 is subject to the *RDA*, any inconsistency between 'rights and interests conferred by native title', which survive the grant of the pastoral lease, and 'rights conferred under the statutory grant' cannot be any more resolved by asserting that the former must yield than by asserting that the latter must yield. Obviously the former can be limited by the grant of the latter, provided the grant occurred prior to the passage of the *RDA*. Can the pastoralist proceed at some time in the future with the building of the house without consulting the native title holders and without compensating them? Under the law as it stood post-*Wik*, he could proceed with legal certainty only with the consent of the native title holders. The majority reasoning in the earlier *Native Title Act* case and the view of the minority in the *Wik* case raised serious legal doubt, doubt which was not necessarily sown by ideological scaremongering legal advice.

There is a need for Commonwealth legislation enacting the assurance which the Aborigines and their legal advisers was offered to pastoralists and governments afraid to proceed with regular development and diversification activities. Two weeks after the *Wik* decision, the Queensland government announced a freeze on all such applications. Some Aboriginal supporters thought this announcement was scaremongering. There may have been a mixed political agenda. But cautious legal advice supported the need for a legislative remedy before developments could be assured validity.

The surprise result in *Wik*, the closeness of the decision and its immediate fear-inducing effects brought the reasoning of the majority judges under close scrutiny. Their use of nineteenth-century historical material was open to question. The key choice for the judges was whether a pastoral lease granted a right of exclusive possession subject only to the exceptions set down in the lease, or the lease granted a right only to co-existing possession and use subject to the historically recognised rights of others, including native title holders, to ongoing possession and use. Three members of the majority detailed the communications from Earl Grey, Secretary of State for the Colonies, to Sir Charles FitzRoy, the newly arrived Governor of New South Wales in 1847–48, indicating the intentions of the imperial authorities. But they did not follow up the fate of Grey's directions, which were unpopular among the power elite in the colony moving towards self-government. For example, Justice Kirby quoted Earl Grey's despatch to Sir Charles FitzRoy on 11 February 1848:

> It should be generally understood that Leases granted for this purpose give the grantees only an exclusive right of pasturage for their cattle, and of cultivating such Land as they may require within the large limits thus assigned to them, but that these Leases are not intended to deprive the Natives of their former right to hunt over these Districts, or to wander over them in search of subsistence, in the manner to which they have been heretofore accustomed, from the spontaneous produce of the soil except over land actually cultivated or fenced in for that purpose.

Neither he nor other members of the majority quoted Grey's further instruction to FitzRoy in that despatch:

> If therefore the limitation which I have mentioned above on the right of exclusive occupation granted by Crown Leases is not, in your opinion, fully recognised in the Colony, I think it is advisable that you should enforce it by some public declaration, or if necessary, by passing a declaratory Enactment.

There was never any public declaration nor Enactment to this effect. Justice Gaudron quoted two other despatches from Earl Grey to similar effect. Her Honour then noted, 'No declaration of that kind found its way into the Order in Council which eventually issued'. Dr Heather Goodall in *Invasion to Embassy* explains why: 'By the time Grey sought to influence the colonies on native title to land there was firm resistance from the squatters against the humanitarian meddling in colonial affairs'.

Two Orders in Council under the *Sale of Waste Lands Act Amendment Act 1846* were issued in 1847 and 1849. According to Justice Kirby: 'These developments provide the common starting point for the evolution of Crown leasehold tenure, including pastoral leases, in what are now the States of New South Wales, Queensland, Victoria and Tasmania'. But, as Queensland argued in the *Wik* proceedings, these Orders in Council simply allowed the governor in his discretion to include a condition for continued Aboriginal access in future pastoral leases. Though a clause permitting Aboriginal access was inserted in some early Queensland pastoral leases, there was never a binding requirement that such clauses be included. It was a matter for the governor's discretion. The Orders in Council were repealed by the parliament of the new colony a year after its separation from New South Wales. Thereafter, even the discretion to insert an access clause was removed. Unlike Western Australia, South Australia and the Northern Territory, the other States did not maintain reservations of Aboriginal access rights to pastoral leases. Neither the legislation nor the leases considered in *Wik* contained any reservations.

Justice Kirby listed 19 Queensland Acts 'with provisions for, or affecting, pastoral leases'. According to Kirby: 'Most of the statutes contained express provisions conferring rights on third parties over a pastoral lease, inconsistent with the submission that the lease conferred rights of exclusive possession upon the lessee'. Justice Toohey said 'they reflected a regime designed to meet a situation that was unknown in England, namely the occupation of large tracts of land unsuitable for residential but suitable for pastoral purposes'. On the other hand, the minority saw these statutory provisions as legislated exceptions to the right of exclusive possession. No member of the majority turned up any Queensland Act or later lease which contained a provision legislating or stating the Earl Grey understanding of continued Aboriginal access. Justice Gaudron said:

> There is nothing to suggest that a right of exclusive possession was either a necessary or convenient feature of pastoral leases in the conditions of the Colony of New South Wales in 1847. And there is nothing to suggest that subsequent statutory measures culminating in the 1910 Act effected any significant change with respect to the estate or interest which they conferred.

But then again, there is nothing to indicate colonial compliance with Earl Grey's fervent wish that the peculiarly Australian pastoral leases explicitly permit continued Aboriginal access.

The majority held that pastoral leases granted pursuant to statutes passed by the legislatures of the self-governing territories were not leases in the common law sense, there being no clear importation of imperial common law lease notions. Rather, pastoral leases were bundles of statutory rights permitting continued Aboriginal access in accordance with the wishes of the imperial authorities. These findings of the majority are difficult to reconcile with the specific wording and political context of the post-1849 Orders in Council and later statutory provisions resulting from the first deliberations of the colonial legislatures armed with the power to create these unique bundles of rights known as pastoral leases. The new conditions to Crown leases were never drafted. Historian Heather Goodall says:

> By late 1849 FitzRoy had his land administrators' support, and the power by Grey's second Order in Council to impose limitations on Crown leases. The squatters, however, continued to be bitterly opposed to any form of recognition of Aboriginal rights to land use.

The squatters got their way. The limitations were never included in the leases.

According to the *Wik* majority, a colonial pastoral lease is not a lease, despite the language of the legislature, because it is a unique statutory instrument, with many variants, to be interpreted according to its terms, not according to preconceptions imported from imperial precedents. But paradoxically this unique colonial statutory instrument does carry with it a right of Aboriginal access, not because of the language of the instrument (which in all its variants in eastern jurisdictions says nothing of such a right) but because of the fervent imperial desires of Earl Grey. The one member of the majority who did not make use of the historical material up to and including the despatches of Earl Grey was Justice Gummow who observed:

> There remains lacking, at least in Australia, any established taxonomy to regulate such uses of history in the formulation of legal norms. Rather, lawyers have 'been bemused by the apparent continuity of their heritage into a way of

> thinking which inhibits historical understanding'. Even if any such taxonomy were to be devised, it might then be said of it that it was but a rhetorical device devised to render past reality into a form useful to legally principled resolution of present conflicts.

In other words, Gummow was doubting that historical material could deliver the answer to the legal quandary. Even less could an incomplete reading of the history yield a satisfying answer.

The reasoning of the *Wik* majority created one other major uncertainty about native title being able to revive on land which previously had been subject to a Crown grant. When a pastoral lease or any other statutorily based land grant expires, the Crown does not necessarily become the full beneficial owner of the land. Native title may be revived. This new proposition of law gives native title far greater scope for present day survival than did the judgments in *Mabo*.

For example, Justice Kirby was very dismissive of the previously entertained notion that the grant of a lease would automatically require the reversion of the full beneficial interest in the land to the Crown at the end of the lease. He said:

> To invent the notion, not sustained by the actual language of the Land Acts, that the power conferred on the Crown to grant a pastoral leasehold interest was an indirect way of conferring on the Crown 'ownership' of the land by means of the reversion expectant involves a highly artificial importation of feudal notions into Australian legislation.

Rather than piling 'fiction upon fiction', he saw no need 'to import the paraphernalia of English feudal leasehold notions'. So in *Wik*, Australian property law moved well beyond the position of Justices Deane and Gaudron in *Mabo* who observed: 'If the slate were clean, there would be something to be said for the view that the English system of land law was not, in 1788, appropriate for application to the circumstances of a British penal colony'. They went on to say that 'the practical effect of the vesting of radical title in the Crown was merely to enable the English system of private ownership of estates held of the Crown to be observed in the Colony'.

Between *Mabo* and *Wik*, the slate was wiped clean by a new majority of the court. No good purpose is to be served by downplaying the magnitude of the Aboriginal double win: the co-existence of native title on pastoral leases which do not provide a lessee with a right of exclusive possession was confirmed, and it was established that the beneficial interest in the land does not revert to the Crown on termination of a lease. But this double win was sure to increase pressure on government to devise a legislative guarantee that native title was extinguished on land grants which did give a right of exclusive possession. Rather than awaiting court decisions about every form of title, it was inevitable that State governments as the primary land administrators would want to draw up a list of exclusive tenures and be assured permanent extinguishment of native title on such lands.

One can still be a strong supporter of Aboriginal rights and an advocate of the political imperative *Wik* provides for land justice while conceding reservations about the court's judicial method. If ever there was a need for joint judgments, it was in this case. Here we have a four–three decision, with all four of the majority writing separate judgments. Meanwhile, the minority signed off on one judgment confining judicial method to an assessment only of the statute and legal instrument called a 'lease'. The majority judges considered a variety of other factors, including a distinctive reading of the history up until 1849 which was taken, at least by Justices Toohey and Kirby, to be foundational, despite the lack of what Justice Gummow described as an 'established taxonomy to regulate such uses of history in the formulation of legal norms'. A consensual majority approach to reasoning as well as outcome would have contributed to certainty.

The majority's failure to address the relationship between the *RDA* and the co-existence of subsidiary native title rights left unresolved the effect of the judgment. The *RDA* usually operates to ensure that rights enjoyed by one racial group are accorded the same protection as the rights enjoyed by any other group. The *RDA* cannot operate in this way on native title rights which have to yield to prevailing pastoral rights. The confusion between the law of extinguishment by Crown grant and the fact of extinguishment by action of a lessee rendered the decision so uncertain as to be unworkable without complementary legislation. These matters were susceptible of ready parliamentary resolution restoring certainty and consistency to the law. The judgment provided not just the opportunity but the necessity for Parliament to address the land entitlements of Aborigines on others' pastoral leases. The moral necessity for legislative action striking the right balance between fairness for Aborigines and certainty and workability for statutory land holders was highlighted by the dissenting three judges' observation:

> The principles of the law may thus be thought to reveal 'a significant moral shortcoming' which can be rectified only by legislation or by the acquisition of an estate which would allow the traditions and customs of the Wik and Thayorre Peoples to be preserved and observed. Those avenues of satisfaction draw on the certainty of proprietary rights created by the sovereign power.

In the *Wik* debate, the principles relating to native title on pastoral leases have been clear. Pastoralists and miners who use land for commercial purposes need and deserve certainty. Aborigines who have maintained their connection with their land are as entitled as any other Australian land holders to legal protection of their rights. Extinguishment of private property rights should be permitted only in the public interest, not for the private gain of others. In modern Australia, we no longer tolerate discrimination against people on the basis of race. Where the principles conflict, there is a need for negotiated compromise and just legislation in the national interest.

If native title exists on a pastoral lease, a miner may have to identify native title holders and deal with them as well as with the pastoralist. Under the unamended *NTA*, the Aborigines would have had a right to negotiate even at the exploration phase. The pastoralist would have had only the right to compensation for disturbance to land.

Native title may be wiped out by developments on a pastoral lease such as the building of houses, dams, fences, roads and sheds. Could these things be done without the permission of the native title holders? Ought there be a need to negotiate? Would the native title holders be entitled to compensation? Who should pay? If native title holders have a right of access to a pastoral lease, are there any limits on the exercise of that right? Can they come without permission from the pastoralist to collect bush tucker? Can they come in vehicles, with guns, with alcohol, with friends, with miners? If native title holders have a right to camp, hunt and fish, are there any limits to the exercise of that right? Can they set up camp for a long time? Can they hunt for commercial gain or in a manner which threatens the commercial entitlements of the pastoralist? Do native title holders have the right to build their own outstations, to run their own pastoral operation, to set up tourist resorts? Do pastoralists have the right to expand their land use from merely pastoral purposes, requiring a right of exclusive possession? For example if they want to run a major tourist operation, do they have to negotiate their change of tenure with native title holders? These were some of the questions confronting the Howard government in the wake of the *Wik* decision. Inevitably the government response would be within the parameters of the changes to the *NTA* which had been flagged in the first nine months of the Howard government coming to terms with the complexity of native title.

State governments, believing native title to be extinguished on pastoral leases, had issued thousands of new interests in land since the *NTA* without going through the processes for negotiating with native title holders. Those interests may have been invalid. As in 1993, there would be a need for a legislative regime validating such grants. But this time there would be nothing on offer to Aboriginal groups to offset this political loss and concession in the negotiation process. There would not even be the prospect of meaningful negotiation. This time, the Aboriginal win in the High Court had little chance of being translated into a win on the floor of Parliament.

6 | THE TEN POINT PLAN 1997

During the 1996 Christmas holiday period, Prime Minister Howard retired to Hawks Nest, his long-time family holiday spot. Tim Fischer took the reins as Acting Prime Minister, flying around the country and fuelling anxiety about the effects of the *Wik* decision. The Queensland government announced a freeze on all land development applications claiming 'the situation was far worse than that stated by those who were playing it down and saying there was nothing to worry about'. Aborigines took the initiative and hosted a *Wik* summit at a resort outside Cairns. Industry and government representatives were invited. Aboriginal leaders put an offer on the table. They would proclaim a self-imposed moratorium on native title claims over pastoral leases provided governments agreed to the non-extinguishment of native title on pastoral leases and undertook to honour the *RDA*. The Prime Minister returned from holidays and immediately laid the groundwork for reversing his previous commitments to honour the common law rights of native title holders and to work within the confines of the *RDA*. Appearing on Channel Nine's *Today* programme, he said: 'There's no law in Australia which is so sacrosanct that it can never be changed. So we mustn't get hung up on this idea that you can never ever, ever amend the *Racial Discrimination Act* or never ever overturn a High Court decision'. Extinguishment was an option. The Queensland National Party wanted the option to extinguish native title on pastoral leases whenever the pastoralist requested an upgrade of tenure, even if the major reason for the upgrade was simply the extinguishment of native title.

The newly emerging National Indigenous Working Group (NIWG) became the lead organisation putting the indigenous perspective. The NIWG is a free-wheeling broadly inclusive group with membership drawn from four national organisations: ATSIC, the Indigenous Land Corporation, the office of the Aboriginal and Torres Strait Islander Social Justice Commissioner and the National Aboriginal and Islander Legal Services Secretariat. These groups are joined by the key representative bodies which have statutory roles under the *NTA*. After meetings with the Prime Minister and consultations around the country, the NIWG issued its little yellow book, entitled *Coexistence—Negotiation and Certainty*, in April 1997. The NIWG set down three policy demands which were unacceptable to the Howard government. They wanted a national framework for local and regional agreements, with representative bodies being one-stop shops which could process agreements for native title claimants and be the preferred channel for negotiations with developers. They demanded that they retain guaranteed access to the National Native Title Tribunal. They saw the right to negotiate with mining companies as the key for 'indigenous economic and social development and participation on a full and equal basis in the life of the nation'.

The right to negotiate was identified as achieving three objectives: cultural protection, economic self-empowerment, and control of negative social impacts. The Howard government accepted the mining industry's claim that the industry should not be the primary deliverer of economic self-empowerment to indigenous Australians. It also accepted the miners' argument that a 14 month right to negotiate process armed native title claimants with a *de facto* veto which permitted them to demand an undeserved share in new mining projects. The breakdown of the Century Zinc negotiations in February 1997 was used by the industry as evidence that the right to negotiate was too cumbersome even for those large companies sympathetic to the tenets of the legislation and which were sufficiently well resourced to employ the best Aboriginal negotiators.

Meanwhile the NFF increased the political heat with a series of television advertisements including black and white children playing Twister, and competing with each other for access to the same areas. Donald McGauchie, President of the NFF, claimed: 'During the entire *Wik* debate, Australia's farmers have never asked for anything more than they had before December 23, 1996'. More correctly, they wanted nothing more than what they thought to be their pre-*Wik* entitlements. Mistakenly, they thought their leases were virtually equivalent to freehold. If native title were extinguished on freehold, it should just as surely have been extinguished on their leases. From their perspective, their pre-*Wik* entitlement included the liberty to apply to State governments for an upgrade of their tenure to freehold on payment of a betterment factor. They felt that entitlement should be still available to them even though it might now mean the extinguishment of some surviving native title rights.

The NFF and the government realised that it would be hard to win public sympathy if the uncertainty over *Wik* was seen principally to affect pastoralists whose landholdings would seem vast to suburban television viewers. The 1500 holders of pastoral leases in Queensland whose properties cover half the State would fall in this category. Most farmers are not pastoralists, and most have a right of exclusive possession to their land just as surely as the freeholder of a city block. The NFF deliberately fudged the issue by running advertisements which suggested that all farmers were confronted with uncertainty.

The NFF's pre-*Wik* arrangement with the Coalition was that native title legislation would be amended to guarantee that a pastoralist could diversify and engage in any primary production activity regardless of any native title considerations. State governments would be at liberty to issue whatever was the appropriate form of tenure for a primary production activity. If that meant interference with native title in light of future court decisions, government rather than the pastoralist would pay the compensation.

The NIWG met a couple of times with the Prime Minister in early 1997 and realised that this time they had a hard road to walk. The Hindmarsh Island bridge saga was back before the Parliament. The government had trouble getting its legislation, suspending the operation of the heritage protection legislation, through the Senate. Putting the Senate on notice, the government reintroduced its legislation in such a way that it could be a trigger for a double dissolution. This was a prelude to the parliamentary tactics over *Wik*. The Labor Party rolled over and the Aboriginal groups feared a sell out of their interests by the major political parties. On 15 April 1997 Kim Beazley, after a series of meetings with stakeholders including a dinner with key mining industry leaders, published 'The Opposition's Position on Native Title After *Wik*', conceding 'there is a case to be made for the right to negotiate process applying on a once-only per project basis'. All state premiers, including Bob Carr, the only remaining Labor premier, urged the Prime Minister to draft legislation confirming Paul Keating's understanding that native title was extinguished on valid pastoral leases issued before 1975.

John Howard decided against extinguishment of common law rights. On 28 April 1997, he unveiled to the premiers his Ten Point Plan to resolve *Wik*. He described it as 'the fairest, best, most practicable way of delivering certainty and security to farmers and justice to the Aboriginal community'. There were three factors saving Aborigines from the 1997 *terra nullius* option. It would cost the taxpayer too much. There were some doubts about the Commonwealth Parliament's power to do it. And the Senate, as presently constituted, would not agree because the majority of senators had given in principle recognition to the co-existence of native title on pastoral leases.

Given these doubts, John Howard decided to sweat it out and call the bluff of the premiers, especially Queensland's Rob Borbidge, refusing to extinguish native title across the board on 42 per cent of the Australian continent. Howard said he had not 'completely ruled out extinguishment'. Economic reality held him back from the brink. He was also worried that the High Court as 'currently constituted could well decide that the race power as currently phrased does not support a detrimental act in relation to one particular race within the Australian community'. Over the next week, the Ten Point Plan underwent some modification, in the course of which no copy of it was available for publication.

The ten points were:

1. Validation

Any acts or grants made over non-vacant crown land after the *NTA* and prior to the *Wik* decision would be validated.

2. Confirmation of extinguishment of native title on 'exclusive' tenures

States and Territories would be able to confirm that freehold, residential, commercial and most agricultural leases and existing public works had extinguished native title.

3. Provision of government services

Essential government services would be able to be delivered to the public on native title land without extinguishing native title.

4. Native title and pastoral leases

State governments would be able to authorise primary production activity and farmstay tourism on pastoral leases regardless of the existence of native title. Native title would not be extinguished but suppressed for the duration of the activity. Compensation would be payable by the State, not the pastoralist.

5. Statutory access rights
Registered native title claimants who had maintained physical access to pastoral lease land at the time of the *Wik* decision would obtain legislative confirmation of their rights of access. Access rights under State laws and leases would be maintained.

6. Future mining activity
There would be a higher threshold test for gaining access to the right to negotiate. On vacant crown land, the right to negotiate would be cut back to a once-only right. On pastoral leases, the right to negotiate could be removed by the State provided that native title holders had the same procedural rights as the pastoral lessee.

7. Future government and commercial development
The right to negotiate would not be available to native title claimants within town and city boundaries. Neither would it be available for compulsory acquisition of land required for infrastructure development.

8. Management of water resources and airspace
The ability of governments to regulate and manage surface and subsurface water, aquatic resources and airspace would be put beyond doubt.

9. Management of claims
States would be encouraged to process native title claims through their own systems. There would be a six year sunset clause. Existing claims, as well as new claims, would be put through a new threshold test.

10. Agreements
Legal certainty would be guaranteed for voluntary agreements about native title, thus providing a real incentive to follow this approach.

Though the NIWG had strong objections to most of the plan, points 1, 3, 8 and 10 were acceptable to the majority of parliamentarians and commentators. The detail of the other points highlighted the Prime Minister's claim that the pendulum had swung too far in favour of Aborigines and he wanted to bring it back to the middle, stripping back Aboriginal gains which had been made in the courts and in the 1993 legislation.

There was provision for the validation of intermediate period actions which were all actions by State governments affecting native title interests between the passage of the *NTA* and the *Wik* judgment. Government wanted to give ironclad certainty to all persons granted titles to land prior to the *Wik* decision, even if government acted as if native title could not exist on pastoral leases. The validation proposal was similar to the 1993 scheme for validation of titles. Given that the NNTT would not even permit the registration of a native title claim over pastoral leases which were without reservations (such as most of the leases in

Queensland) until February 1996, State governments could hardly be blamed for not following the processes of the Act.

Government and the NIWG were agreed that there should be legislative backing for indigenous land use agreements which would encourage local and regional agreements among all stakeholders concerned about future actions on native title land.

In the light of the Yorta Yorta claim and some extravagant demands by representative bodies purporting to prevent normal shire council functions pending the finalisation of regional agreements, government also wanted to be able to deliver ordinary municipal services and to regulate water and air space with certainty and without native title complications. Any interference with native title would be compensated on just terms. In some parts of Australia, the new, inexperienced land councils sponsored ambit claims over all sorts of titles. Taking their lead from the Yorta Yorta precedent, they claimed exclusive possession, occupation and use of the land 'as against the whole world'. These claims were drafted by lawyers who simply adopted the wording of the court order in the *Mabo* case, which related to land where no one else lived. Pastoralists in remote areas without access to their own lawyers were horrified to receive letters asserting such claims. Those claims were now to be put through a closer sieve. The legislation would confirm complete extinguishment of native title not just on freehold but on any other tenures which carried an automatic right of upgrading to freehold. This would meet the concerns of farmers and most graziers who held titles such as the Queensland grazing homestead freehold leases and agricultural farm leases. These would be as free from native title claim as the city freehold block. They always were safe under *Mabo* and *Wik*. But given the antics of Premier Borbidge about the High Court and judicial theft, the Parliament was to make clear the common law situation.

The only titleholders whose land could be subject to co-existing native title were those who did not have a right to upgrade to freehold and whose tenure was non-exclusive. Usually these are the holders of pastoral leases. In Western Australia, South Australia and the Northern Territory, these leaseholders have always had to permit some Aboriginal access. In New South Wales, Aborigines denied access have had recourse to the Land and Environment

Court for a permit. Only in Queensland did Aboriginal access to pastoral leases come as a totally new suggestion for the 1500 pastoralists whose sheep and cattle roam over half the State. The Commonwealth government adopted the catalogue of rights agreed by the pastoralists and Aborigines in the Cape York Land Agreement and proposed making those rights available to any registered claimants who regularly had physical access to the land. There was understandable Aboriginal concern about how this provision would prejudice any native title claimants who had previously been locked out from pastoral properties or who had been moved by State officials without consent.

The National Party insisted that Howard face the bush and sell his plan, which was more complex than their preferred one point plan of extinguishment. The night before Howard and Fischer spoke at the Stockman's Hall of Fame in Longreach, Fischer told national radio: 'There are bucketfuls of extinguishment in the ten point plan'. The feisty National Party backbencher Senator Bill O'Chee had earlier claimed: 'We've now got the situation where native title will be extinguished one way or another on private property. All we are now really arguing over is who pays compensation and how much'. In the public exchanges between the Liberals and Nationals, the choice had not been between extinguishment and co-existence but between extinguishment up front, the blanket variety, and extinguishment by the back door, which came in buckets.

The Ten Point Plan allowed States to extinguish native title on pastoral leases so that pastoralists could be given upgraded freehold title. When Pat Dodson took exception to this proposal at the Australian Reconciliation Convention, the Prime Minister lost his temper and shouted: 'I, in the name of truth and in the name of a frank discussion of these issues have to repudiate the claim that my ten point plan involves a massive handout of freehold title at taxpayer expense. That is an absolute myth. It is absolutely contrary to the facts and I absolutely repudiate it'. When Malcolm Fraser urged the government to drop this part of the proposed legislation, Senator Nick Minchin replied that Fraser did not understand the measure. Fraser understood all too well. Howard wanted the Commonwealth Parliament to roll back the operation of the *RDA* so that Rob Borbidge would be free to act in a racially discriminatory way wiping out proven native title rights, not for a public purpose but for the convenience of a pastoralist with a lease on native title land. The city taxpayers would be left to pick up the tab. Minchin argued that continued Commonwealth insistence that States not be permitted to act in this racially discriminatory way 'would represent a massive intrusion by the Commonwealth into the land management responsibilities of State governments'. Western Australia's Richard Court was prepared to accept racially non-discriminatory non-extinguishment of native title provided native title holders did not retain a right to negotiate with mining companies on pastoral lease lands.

The NIWG branded the government's working draft of the legislation as 'the final theft'. State governments were engaged in furious horse trading about the list of exclusive tenures which could be guaranteed by legislation to have extinguished native title. The Commonwealth government insisted that the confirmation regime 'would reflect the current state of the common law'. If reputable legal opinion was agreed that a particular title granted a right of exclusive possession, it could be listed. Non-controversial listings included town leases and most farming tenures such as agricultural leases. Western Lands leases in New South Wales were not eligible because there were conflicting opinions by QCs about the effect of those leases. The New South Wales Farmers produced a number of legal opinions, two of which came from lawyers who had been quite critical of the High Court in earlier public addresses. The farmers were adamant that their leases were over far smaller and much more developed and closely settled areas than those considered by the court in *Wik*. The *Wik* leases covered completely undeveloped areas of land in remote locations, one covering hundreds of square miles. The farmers took heart from Justice Kirby's observation that the *Wik* leases (unlike theirs in western New South Wales) were 'a far cry from the situation in settled and occupied areas of Australia where the extinguishment of native title has a practical and necessary quality'. The farmers claimed that the term 'exclusive occupation', which had sounded falsely in Justice Kirby's ears when applied to the land covered by the *Wik* leases, rang true for their much smaller, fenced and improved lease areas in much more closely settled regions. The New South Wales government produced a contrary opinion from John McCarthy

QC who had acted for the New South Wales government in the Dunghutti claim at Crescent Head, the first native title claim to be determined and registered on the Australian mainland. The absence of Western Lands leases from the schedule of exclusive tenures does not mean native title does or even can exist on any such lease. The issue awaits court determination.Given that the leases are perpetual, granted for the exclusive benefit of the lessee, and available for a diversity of activities, it is highly likely that the courts will rule that a Western Lands lease grants a right of exclusive possession.

While Premier Carr was prepared to defer to legal doubt and leave the matter to the courts, Rob Borbidge in Queensland was anxious to have all tenures except pastoral holdings listed in the schedule of exclusive titles. Under Queensland legislation, there is a vast array of these tenures, many of which do grant exclusive occupation and carry an automatic right of upgrade to freehold. One such tenure is the 'grazing homestead freeholding lease' which came to prominence as the title held by the family of Camilla Cowley, who incurred the wrath of the NFF when she took a public stand in favour of native title, establishing a 'Landholders for Co-existence' group. She came on to the national stage when she was photographed in the midst of the Sea of Hands with Gladys Tybingoompa, the Wik elder who had danced outside the High Court when the decision was handed down. Camilla Cowley's critics pointed out that her property had been freeholded. The legal monkey of native title was now off her back, and she could enter into a voluntary access agreement. But many pastoralists resented her voluntary generosity being quoted by city supporters to force pastoralists to accept co-existence of title on non-exclusive tenures. By July 1997, Borbidge was confident that the State's 3000 grazing homestead perpetual leases would be included in the schedule even though the State minister could reject an application for freeholding of such tenures if the Land Administration Commission certified that public interests would be adversely affected.

The Aboriginal groups were particularly concerned about the capacity granted to State governments to authorise a diversity of primary production activity on pastoral leases. This concern was overstated, given the complex legal provisions which already existed in each State permitting some agricultural activity on pastoral leases even without ministerial consent. Take for example the *Wik* leases themselves. Since 1986, all pastoral lessees in Queensland have been authorised by statute to use their holding 'for pastoral or agricultural purposes or for such other purpose as the Minister has first approved in writing'.

The centrepiece of the Ten Point Plan was the government's commitment to remove completely the right to negotiate with mining companies from native title claimants whose land was subject to pastoral lease. Native title holders on vacant crown land would retain a once only right to negotiate. Government would have the power to stop negotiations and authorise an immediate development that would have substantial economic benefit for the country. The State minister would also have the power to step in and suspend consideration of a development application by the arbitral body. There would be no right to negotiate for infrastructure developments such as the Teneco pipeline. Neither would the right to negotiate be available to native title holders inside town and city boundaries.

On 31 July 1997, the High Court gave judgment in the *Stolen Generations* case. Justice Gummow, the one member of the *Wik* majority who did not use questionable historical arguments to buttress his finding that a pastoral lease did not grant a right of exclusive possession subject only to exceptions defined in the lease or legislation, said:

> Before federation the common law as it applied in the Australian colonies had been, as the common law in Australia is now, in continuing development by the courts administering it. In the nature of things, from time to time legislatures perceive the common law as unsatisfactory and as requiring, in a particular aspect, abrogation or modification. Thus the doctrines of common employment and of contributory negligence propounded in English nineteenth-century decisions and the state of the law before the *Married Women's Property Act 1882* (UK) invited and received legislative intervention. Other instances might readily be given.

Indeed they might. One that came readily to mind was *Wik*. The High Court had defined the common law rights. It was now for the

Parliament to abrogate or modify the common law within the constraints of constitutional power. When challenged after the second *Wik* debate in the Senate, Prime Minister Howard told journalists: 'We are doing what governments from time immemorial have done and that is that if the law, as declared by the courts is, in the view of government, in need of change then we seek to change it'.

On 12 August 1997, Gareth Evans told the NFF Council that Labor would not countenance 'the removal of the native title holders' rights to negotiate, especially in the context of mining interests given the economic empowerment that the present right entails'. Until then, Kim Beazley had restricted himself to general observations about the need for certainty for all players—Aborigines, pastoralists, miners, shire councils and taxpayers. The Labor Party had firmed its support for the indigenous position with a coalition of support between the Left of the party, always supportive of Aboriginal aspirations, and the New South Wales Right, which was anxious to maintain the Keating patrimony of 1993. The showdown would come in the Senate over the right to negotiate. Until Evans' speech to the NFF, the miners were hopeful that the Labor leadership would adopt their line of reasoning and agree to the scaling back of the right to negotiate.

With the tabling of his legislation on 4 September 1997, John Howard decided to go in hard on the right to negotiate. He appeared on the ABC's *7.30 Report* that night and produced a graphic map of Australia courtesy of the NFF. He said to the interviewer:

> Let me just show your viewers that this shows 78 per cent of the land mass of Australia—coloured brown on the map. Now, the Labor Party and the Democrats are effectively saying that the Aboriginal people of Australia should have the potential right of veto over further development of 78 per cent of the land mass of Australia.

The kernel of truth in the Prime Minister's presentation was that 78 per cent of the Australian land mass is not subject to exclusive tenure. Native title could exist on such land if Aborigines had still maintained their connection with the land. They would then have a right to negotiate with a mining company, but they would not have a veto over mining development.

Community support in the cities was building with groups such as ANTaR (Australians for Native Title and Reconciliation). Full page advertisements appeared in newspapers calling for co-existence and negotiation. Public rallies took place in most urban centres. The Sea of Hands with over 60,000 plastic hands each bearing the name of a native title supporter toured the country. ANTaR grew out of the call for a People's Movement made by Patrick Dodson at the conclusion of the Reconciliation Convention. ANTaR was unequivocally committed to supporting the policy position of the NIWG. Senator Nick Minchin took strong exception to well known citizens joining the call for co-existence and non-extinguishment. He wrote to signatories of the advertisements insisting that the Ten Point Plan's provision permitting upgrade of pastoral titles was 'only possible in strict accordance with the *Racial Discrimination Act*'. He thought the conveners of ANTaR were 'misrepresenting the truth on native title and the Government's proposals'.

The Prime Minister entertained leading industry executives at the Lodge who were then convinced to put their name to an advertisement endorsing in very general terms the government's legislative solution to *Wik*. None of the leaders was available for interview. The Minerals Council of Australia maintained a low profile. At one stage its President, Nick Stump, indicated that the industry could live with a once-only right to negotiate exercisable by native title holders who had passed a strict threshold test even if their country be subject to pastoral lease. But the press gallery was assured this was a slip up. AMEC (the Western Australia-based Association of Mining and Exploration Companies which takes a more blunt approach to the political process than the Canberra-based MCA) went in boots and all, describing the right to negotiate as 'quite specious' in its submission to the Parliamentary Joint Committee on Native Title. AMEC was known to have the ear of Premier Richard Court. Noting that over 70 per cent of Western Australian mineral production occurred on pastoral lease land, AMEC said:

> There is simply no room to negotiate on the matter. The right to negotiate has delivered to Aboriginal claimants a *de facto* veto and that is over a

> community resource. It is not a resource which is held by any one segment of the community. As an industry, we no longer intend to labour under that sort of disability.

Pleading for the small and medium sized companies, AMEC claimed they 'cannot afford the compliance costs associated with native title'. The MCA followed up, claiming there was plenty of evidence that the right to negotiate was used as 'a *de facto* veto, in the sense that negotiations have been under duress to the point where companies will pay more than what we would consider to be a normal fair outcome to get on with it'.

The South Australian Liberal government conceded in its submission to the committee that a sunset clause was a political gimmick. Denying access to the right to negotiate for unregistered native title claimants after six years was 'unlikely to prove particularly significant in practice'. The Commonwealth parliamentary committee was hopelessly divided along party lines. The Labor Party was acting as if it were still in government. It proposed over 350 amendments. Beazley once referred to 'our Bill', as compared with the government's. Gareth Evans wrote to one community group pledging his party's non-compromising stance against the government's 'legally and morally indefensible assault on the right to negotiate'. Committing the party to the fundamental rights and interests of native title holders, he said: 'The Australian Labor Party is totally committed to achieving this result, and if we cannot we will vote against the whole legislative package, whatever the political consequences'. Labor had drawn its bottom line. Presumably the political consequences included the prospect of a double dissolution election.

When outlining the detail of the Labor position at a national press conference a week later, Daryl Melham, the Shadow Minister for Aboriginal Affairs, was asked about a double dissolution. He replied: 'That's not our decision. That's a matter for the government. But I think it's fair to say that both Kim Beazley and Gareth Evans have already said, "If that is what John Howard wants in the end, then that's a matter for him"'. Putting forward its 350 amendments, the ALP portrayed itself as the credible alternative government, with Nick Bolkus who had the carriage of the matter in the Senate saying:

> Now we reckon that this is the only workable package in town at the moment. The Government's package is one that is looking very, very shaky in a whole range of ways, and we'll proceed with other parties in the Senate, and we'd like to get the Government to rethink their position.

Bolkus told the media: 'We expect to have the numbers in respect to an overwhelming proportion of our ideas and our concepts'. There was little room for compromise.

In the lead-up to the first Senate debate, government–Aboriginal relations took another nose dive with the government confirming there would be no parliamentary apology for the plight of the Stolen Generations. Pat Dodson decided to bow out as Chair of the Council for Aboriginal Reconciliation. Tensions were evident even at the state funeral for Nugget Coombs, with Pat Dodson's proposed eulogy causing offence to the Prime Minister. Paul Keating emerged from self-imposed isolation to defend the balance struck by his legislation in 1993.

7 THE SENATE AND THE STICKING POINTS 1997–98

By the time the *Native Title Amendment Bill* reached the Senate for the first time in November 1997, relations between the indigenous leaders and the Howard government were at breaking point. Noel Pearson lashed out: 'These people who've concocted the ten point scam, who call themselves true liberals, are not true liberals. They are racist scum'. Some saw this outburst as a timely wake-up call to the nation; others saw it as Pearson's disqualification from participation in the forthcoming debate. John Howard told his party room of covenants with miners and pastoralists that needed to be honoured. There was no suggestion of a covenant with the Aborigines. The government's major objective was to cut back the statutory right to negotiate with mining companies. This was to be done by stressing that the right to negotiate was not a common law right recognised by the High Court, but an added statutory right conferred by Parliament in 1993 when it was presumed that native title did not exist on pastoral leases. The government needed a credible argument for distinguishing native title holders whose lands were 'vacant crown land' and those whose lands were subject to pastoral lease. They said the right to negotiate should not be enjoyed by native title holders who would never have a right of exclusive access and use. As those on pastoral leases would have at best co-existing rights, they should have only the same rights as the pastoralist.

The government knew they confronted two sets of critics in the community. There were the outright opponents of the Ten Point Plan. They would be treated as Labor sympathisers who had not got used to the idea that there had been a change of government. Then there were those critics who accepted that the government had the right and duty to govern, but who wanted to take issue with particular provisions of the plan on the basis that it had not struck the right balance, failing to treat equally and decently all parties including Aborigines. In the lead-up to the first Senate debate, the government response to this second set of critics included a frontal attack on the church leaders.

Warren Entsch, a robust pastoralist from north Queensland who chairs the Parliamentary Joint Committee on Native Title, led the charge. After Entsch called for a boycott of churches, the Prime Minister stepped up to the dispatch box not with a hose to douse the Entsch bushfire but with a fan:

> May I say of my colleague the member for Leichhardt that I understand his sense of frustration—and the sense of frustration of many people in rural Australia—about the way in which this debate is being conducted. I do not support a call for a boycott of church attendance, but I can understand the sense of frustration he feels.

This was preceded by the Prime Minister's recitation of the written code for 'church figures' who wish to avail themselves of the right of free speech: 'The right to speak freely on a broad range of issues carries with it the obligation to speak in an informed, objective and constructive fashion'. This was fairly gratuitous, especially coming from the key participant in the debate who had so muddied the waters with the map on television falsely claiming 78 per cent of Australia could be subject to an Aboriginal veto.

John Howard then went to Vancouver for an APEC meeting and left Tim Fischer in charge. The Anglican archbishops of Perth and Adelaide had been taken to task by an Anglican vicar from Charleville, Queensland. The Acting Prime Minister thought it worthwhile giving Parliament the vicar's assessment: 'There are three words that could describe the comments made by the archbishops. The first word is ignorant; the second word is uncaring; and the third word is hypocritical'. Fischer's own comment was: 'That is the church leader I support in relation to *Wik* and *Mabo*'. John Howard's code was being liberally interpreted in his absence.

It was important for the government to silence the churches because the decision had been taken not to compromise on the key provisions of the 300 page Bill proposed to Parliament. In being so unwilling to compromise, government still wanted to be seen to be acting decently. The government knew it would be difficult to reject reasoned, constructive suggestions which enjoyed community backing, including from church leaders, unless there were a concerted campaign against all critics, including the churches. For a touch of spice, there would also be one last suggestion that the backyards were under threat, salvageable only by an unamended Ten Point Plan. The crunch issue was the right to negotiate. Aboriginal negotiators were adamant that this issue was non-negotiable, a right to negotiate being much less than a veto. Rather than acknowledging this right, the Prime Minister took to describing it as simply 'a special arrangement entered into by the former government'.

The NIWG had developed a close working relationship with the minor parties in the Senate, which were prepared to take their riding instructions from them. The ALP had firmed in its resolve to put an alternative legislative package, considering that on such a key policy issue it had a responsibility as the alternative government to set down its position in some detail. The NIWG had retained the services of Warren Snowden, ex-ALP member for the Northern Territory in the House of Representatives. The NIWG had the services of two QCs—John Basten and Ron Castan, who were also available to the ALP. Ron Castan had been called in because of his good working relationship with Gareth Evans. Though Shadow Treasurer and no longer in the Senate, Evans came to play a key role in shaping Labor's exhaustive set of amendments and in selling them to the public. It was inconceivable that the Howard government would dump its own legislation and embrace a legislative package designed by the architects of the 1993 legislation of which the new government was so critical. But the NIWG, Labor and the minor parties took their stand and said they could do no other. Later they were to strenuously reject my public suggestion that their strategy was posited on a post-election legislative outcome. They said they did not want a double dissolution. They just wanted the government to accept their Bill.

Prior to the commencement of the first Senate debate, the Prime Minister hosted another dinner at the Lodge for business executives. *Wik* dominated the agenda. Thirty of Australia's most respected business leaders then issued a statement demanding that the Senate pass the Bill. The mining industry commenced a national advertising campaign asking the Senate to pass the Bill before Christmas. The ads were headed: 'Please don't block opportunities for Australia by prolonging the *Wik* debate'.

Because of the numbers in the Senate and the rejection of the government package by the Opposition and the minor parties, Brian Harradine was left as the one man in the middle who would determine the fate of the government's legislation. The cartoonist Nicholson portrayed Harradine as 'the rainbow serpent starting his epic journey to shape the *Wik* landscape'. Harradine spoke of the need for certainty, workability and fairness for all parties. He took the view that the government was entitled to have most of its legislation passed by the Senate. He would not interfere with provisions which the government assured the Senate were certain and workable. But he was prepared to question the government's bottom line on a few key policy issues when it came to fairness and decency for native title holders. He spoke of the need for 'honourable compromise'. He showed his hand at the commencement of the debate, declaring that the legislation 'requires substantial amendment before it passes this chamber'. He spelt out the quandary which was to confront the Senate twice in the coming months:

> At the end of the day, the government will need to consent to the legislation, since whatever happens here will have to go to the House of Representatives. I do hope that, if we take that approach, the government is more likely to hear and ultimately agree. I certainly do not want to see a divisive election, and the prospect of a double dissolution election about this particular matter is something that is concerning me. It is, I believe, a weight on people's minds right around Australia.

He left the door open to the Prime Minister, saying: 'I would hope to be invited around the back by the end of this week'. First time around, the call never came. Harradine was attentive to the hundreds of phone calls and letters from pastoralists wanting to develop their leases. He was sympathetic to miners seeking a more workable registration test and right to negotiate. But he was adamant that native title rights would be protected in a non-discriminatory way, and the right to negotiate enjoyed by all native title holders. Harradine was committed to a legislative solution which would return certainty and workability to pastoralists who wanted to exercise their rights to land use as they had prior to the *Wik* decision. But he insisted that the need for negotiation or vetting by native title claimants remained except in the case of those primary production activities which could have been authorised on a lease before the *Wik* decision. He did not want the *Wik* decision being used as a Trojan horse for wholesale upgrading of pastoral leases to freehold, or for more expansive primary production activity than previously possible, if an increase in pastoralist's rights were to be obtained by a discriminatory extinguishment of any surviving native title rights. Not until 26 November 1997 did the Queensland National Party drop its proposal that the Queensland Parliament legislate to permit the wholesale upgrading of pastoral leases to freehold with a universal extinguishment of native title.

Though agreeable to a stricter threshold test, Harradine wanted to protect native title claimants who had been locked out of pastoral properties either by the actions of the pastoralist or government. Though agreeable to trimming back the right to negotiate with mining companies to a once-only right to negotiate, he insisted that the right be exercisable by all native title holders whether or not their land was subject to a pastoral lease, inside a town or city boundary, in a national park or required for infrastructure development. And he wanted the once-only right to be enjoyed without the prospect of ministerial interference during the discussion and arbitration phases.

Finally, Harradine was insistent that any provision permitting an upgrade of pastoral title would operate in a non-discriminatory way if the upgrade required the extinguishment of native title. He proposed that this part of the legislation be made strictly subject to the *RDA*. Harradine circulated an amendment similar to the Democrats/Greens 1993 amendment which would have ensured strict compliance of that part of the legislation with the *RDA*.

The NIWG/ALP lawyers were concerned that a provision subjecting only one part of the legislation to the *RDA* would allow the courts to determine that other parts of the legislation were not subject to such constraint. These lawyers had been party to the 1993 Senate compromise which produced the formula in the *NTA*: 'Nothing in this Act affects the operation of the *Racial Discrimination Act*.' They proposed that the whole of the 1997 Amendment Act be made strictly subject to the *RDA* while the original Act was not. This would have been very irresponsible, uncertain law making by Parliament, because anyone wanting to read a future copy of the *NTA* would need to know whether a section was passed in 1993 or later. If it were passed in 1993, it would not be subject to the *RDA*; if passed later, it would be. After protracted back room discussions, the ALP was happy to run with an amendment that the whole Act, as amended, was 'intended to be read and construed subject to the provisions of the *Racial Discrimination Act*.' They would not support Democrat and Green amendments that the whole Act, as amended, be 'subject to the *Racial Discrimination Act*'. There was some very esoteric jurisprudential discussion around the corridors of Parliament House about the difference between the two *RDA* amendments. At every turn, there was a new QC opinion. While it was difficult to explain the operation of the first amendment, all lawyers were agreed that the second one was a 'clause buster' because it would render inoperative any provision that worked in a discriminatory way.

During the Senate debate back in 1993, the Labor government was not prepared to accept a proposed amendment by the Democrats that the preamble of the *Native Title Act* state: 'It is the intention of the Parliament that the *Racial Discrimination Act 1975* shall prevail over the provisions of this Act'. Neither were they agreeable to an amendment, proposed by the Aboriginal negotiators, that: 'Nothing in this Act authorises any conduct whether legislative, executive or judicial, that is inconsistent with the operation of the *Racial Discrimination Act*'. Labor had reported to the Senate Standing Committee on Legal and Constitutional Affairs in December 1993:

> The Bill should be amended to make clear that it is the intention of the Parliament that the Bill is consistent with the *RDA* and constitutes a special measure for the advancement of Aboriginal peoples and Torres Strait Islanders.
>
> This should not provide that the Bill is subject to the *RDA* because of the uncertainty that would create—contrary to one of the very basic objectives of the legislation.

Four years later, but this time from the Opposition benches, the same Labor lawyers could not say what substantive benefit their proposed amendment would deliver to native title holders. They insisted the provision was not a 'clause buster'. Like the existing provision it would probably be construed by the courts merely as a construction provision, which assists with the interpretation of ambiguous provisions, rather than a substantive provision that renders inoperative any inconsistent provisions of the *NTA*. It would have symbolic and political value rather than legal effect. They insisted that their amendment was not the same as a provision that the Act be 'subject to the *RDA*'. The government said the Opposition amendment was too uncertain, for the same reasons given by Labor when in government in 1993.

At the end of the first Senate debate, John Howard identified four key sets of amendments which were 'in the eyes of the government, completely unacceptable'. He said the Government would vote against them because they had 'substantially altered the thrust and the intent of the legislation'. The four objectionable sets of amendments were the threshold test, the six year sunset clause, the statutory negotiation process for mining and development projects, and the proposal to subject the *NTA* to the provisions of the *RDA*. The amendments had the support of the ALP, the Democrats, the Greens and Harradine.

Here is a brief analysis of the four sticking points. In this first Senate debate, the government was sympathetic to Senator Harradine's amendment to the **threshold test** which would allow Aborigines locked out of pastoral leases still to lodge a claim. Senator Minchin told the Senate on 1 December 1997: 'We have had a good look at Senator Harradine's amendment and we would be prepared to accept that amendment. In the light of the comments that have been made around the chamber, we think that is a not inappropriate amendment'.

Because of welcome government amendments moved in the Senate, native title claimants would now be able to lodge a claim over their traditional lands which they occupy once any freehold estate or lease had expired and not been renewed. This rendered any **sunset clause** completely arbitrary and unprincipled. The effect of a sunset clause would be to permit a claim over land if the lease were to expire within the next six years, while barring a claim over land were the lease to run out in seven years without any prospect of renewal.

The Prime Minister tried to develop two new arguments for taking away the **right to negotiate** for native title holders on pastoral leases. One was meaningless and the other unprincipled. He said:

> Of the many ironies that are thrown up by this debate, none is stronger than the consequences of the Labor Party's insistence that the right to negotiate in the existing *Native Title Act* be left unaltered by the amendment Bill, because that has two consequences. The first consequence it has is to prevent effect being given to the spirit of the *Wik* decision, because if you leave a right to negotiate there you cannot possibly give effect to the spirit of the *Wik* decision. The second consequence is that you are conferring a right on native title claimants that you are not conferring on pastoralists. So apparently in relation to a mining claim it is perfectly all right for a right to negotiate to be available to native title claimants but it is not all right for it to be available to pastoralists. There is no equity, there is no fairness and there is no justice in that outcome.

The spirit of the *Wik* decision is not that pastoralists necessarily have more or the same rights as native title holders when it comes to dealing with miners. The spirit of the decision is that native title holders retain their rights provided there is no conflict with the rights of the pastoralists. Any conflict of rights between native title holders and pastoralists is resolved in favour of the pastoralists. Nothing in the *Wik* decision relates to mining rights.

As for the second consequence, the Commonwealth Parliament has an obligation to set an appropriate bottom line for relationships between native title holders and miners. The right to negotiate encourages Aborigines and miners to talk together and to work together from the beginning. The Commonwealth Parliament does not have power to make laws about the rights exercisable by pastoral lessees under State titles. The veto, negotiation and compensation rights of farmers affected by mining is a State matter. For example, some farmers in Western Australia whose lands are cultivated and enclosed have a veto over mining development. At the other end of the scale are those pastoralists who have only a right to compensation for disturbance to the land.

In the dying stages of the first Senate debate, there was intense debate on **the *RDA* clause**. The government was adamant that each clause of its legislation was non-discriminatory and that a clause subjecting the whole Bill to the *RDA* would render the legislation so uncertain as to be unworkable. There would be no certainty until the courts had given definitive judgments about the interpretation of each clause that affected the relationship between native title and other rights granted by the Crown. Before lunch on the last day, Harradine explained why he would reject the *RDA* amendment:

> There will be endless litigation about it. Why did we not put it in the 1993 legislation? For the very reason that we ought not be putting it in here. The Labor government at that time knew that it was a nonsense to put a similar provision in the *Native Title Act*. If the Labor Party faced up to the real world now, they would realise that it would be, and is, not an appropriate thing to do if you want to have the legislation work for the benefit of indigenous people—native title holders—and in fairness to the rights of other persons.

After lunch he changed his mind and voted for the *RDA* amendment. Lawyers convinced him over lunch that the *RDA* clause, whatever its effect, would not be a clause buster. By then it was known that Howard would vote down the Senate Bill, while the Opposition would not even give the amended Senate Bill a third reading unless it included the *RDA* amendment. By voting for the uncertain *RDA* amendment, Harradine ensured that there would be an alternative Bill on the books which could form the basis for debate next time around. The Senate Bill contained 217 amendments, 100 of which were government amendments and another 25 of which were acceptable to the government. So there had been some movement, but not enough.

On 6 December 1997, the Prime Minister rejected the Senate Bill and told Parliament of his commitment to find 'an honourable, decent and worthy compromise'. He said: 'In a compromise, you do not surrender to one interest, you try to strike a fair balance'. After this first Senate debate, there were two groups in the country accepting a double dissolution scenario. First, there were those opposed to native title rights being exercised on pastoral leases. They wanted the election so that the Howard government could implement its plan without the full range of Senate amendments. They especially wanted to do away with the right to negotiate with mining companies, except on 'vacant crown land' subject to native title claim. Second, there were the strong advocates of native title who believed that a double dissolution would give the Labor Party a real chance of election with a commitment to a full blooded implementation of the *Wik* decision. The day after Howard rejected the Senate Bill, Beazley said that the Prime Minister was now locked in to his threat of a double dissolution which would be 'a penalty the nation pays for weak government'.

The ALP National Conference in January 1998 resolved that 'Labor will continue to support amendments which ensure that the Act is subject to the provisions of the *RDA*'. But this was not to mean that Labor would vote for Democrat or Green amendments which did subject the Act to the *RDA*. Once again it meant only that Labor would support a Claytons *RDA* clause. They thought it was a stronger Claytons clause than their 1993 version. But they could not say what was its effect.

Once again the Prime Minister holidayed with family at Hawks Nest over the summer and Tim Fischer was given another opportunity to peddle the National Party perspective on native title under the mantle of the acting prime ministership. The party politics was difficult for the Aboriginal groups. They had cancelled a meeting with the Prime Minister before Christmas, causing grave embarrassment to the moderate Gatjil Djerrkura, Chairman of ATSIC, who had made the appointment. There were many mixed messages. In January 1998, I, who regarded the *RDA* discussion as legally esoteric and politically damaging, asked the NIWG if there were any point in agitating for the acceptance of the Senate Bill without the *RDA* amendment. Peter Yu for the NIWG advised that 'such a course would not be helpful and in fact may be harmful to the indigenous position'. The NIWG claimed to be involved with other prominent Aboriginal people in pursuing other options with conservative political interests, and representatives of the Commonwealth and State governments. This would have been news to Tim Fischer, who was crusading around Queensland, beating the *Wik* drum at the beginning of Rob Borbidge's election year. The Coalition government was firmly of the view that the NIWG was playing party politics with little interest in a solution to *Wik*. Noel Pearson, Tracker Tilmouth and Pat Dodson were all being suggested as possible Labor candidates in the next federal election. While Pearson thought he would have access to 'more safe seats than a Volvo', Tilmouth was locked out from the succession to Bob Collins' Senate seat in the Northern Territory, and Pat Dodson declined a personal approach from Kim Beazley, who flew all the way to Broome to convince him. Aden Ridgeway, Executive Director of the New South Wales Aboriginal Land Council, was already an endorsed candidate for the Democrats.

The Aboriginal leaders were convinced the government had shown no capacity for principled compromise. Returning from holidays, John Howard sent a personal letter to hundreds of community leaders enclosing a document entitled 'Fairness and Balance'. It gave stark figures on the unworkability of the existing *NTA:* only two determinations of native title; 669 outstanding applications covering 50 per cent of the continent; 210 million dollars for the administration of the native title regime to date; and a backlog of 7000 mining titles in Western Australia with 1900 of these 'caught up in the *Native Title Act*'s "right to negotiate" process'. Howard then made his first visit as Prime Minister to an Aboriginal community. His host at Yirrkala was Gatjil Djerrkura,who later said: 'Many of my people are thinking, "OK, stuff the government, let's go to an election and let the people decide", but I am a firm believer that sometimes you have to work through the system to win what you want from the system'. At Yirrkala, they discussed the right to negotiate, and Howard said: 'If you can come up with a formula for compromise we'll take that on board and look at it'.

Back in Canberra, the prospect of compromise was slight. However in the back rooms, both sides were looking at how the cultural heritage of native title holders on pastoral leases could be maintained in a self-determining way, even if the Aborigines were denied the limited economic bargaining power attached to the right to negotiate. Up front before the cameras, the government and the NIWG were still eyeballing each other. The NIWG held a national press conference on 11 March 1998 saying they were 'absolutely opposed to a double dissolution'. After three months silence, they wrote that morning to the key stakeholders seeking a roundtable discussion. The MCA labelled it a stunt. The NIWG decided on an uncompromising public stance, saying: 'We don't fall back from our position in regards to the yellow document we released last year as the basis for which we are prepared to negotiate'. They wanted to retain a twofold right to negotiate in all circumstances, and blamed the delay with development applications on the constraints placed on the representative bodies. If government were prepared to make these bodies one-stop shops with power to negotiate regional agreements about past and future acts, most problems would be solved from the NIWG's point of view. This carried no weight with State or Commonwealth governments. For the NIWG, the right to negotiate was non-negotiable. They had drawn their line in the sand. Peter Yu denied that there was any split with Gatjil Djerrkura: 'It's just been a matter of we haven't had the time to meet him and he's been away up bush with the Prime Minister'. Geoff Clarke, the ATSIC Commissioner for Native Title, said the ATSIC board position was 'that we would be maintaining the right to negotiate'. The prospect of a breakthrough was slight. The NFF was nowhere to be seen. Mr McGauchie was down on the waterfront, presumably having closed his *Wik* file, and happy to do the government's bidding on the wharves, content that the government would do his bidding at the farm gate. The miners were quiet. This time the Aborigines had the corridors of Parliament to themselves, though there were State government bureaucrats attending to detail.

Labor's most knowledgeable Senator on Aboriginal issues, Bob Collins, decided not to return to Parliament for the second Senate debate which was due before Easter 1998. He was retiring early. He told *The Age*: 'On the question of the *RDA*, I was identified along with the Frank Brennan camp. But at the end of the day, naturally I would have supported the party's position. There's no way in the world I'm going to rat on the Labor Party'. The second Senate debate was delayed until the High Court delivered judgment in the Hindmarsh Island case, which ruled that the Parliament had constitutional power partially to repeal legislation advantageous to Aborigines. Until then, Labor had taken some heart from legal arguments that any amendments to the *NTA* would themselves have to be beneficial to Aborigines if their constitutional validity was to be put beyond doubt. The Hindmarsh decision fortified the government in its view that Parliament could wind back the right to negotiate regime without running into trouble in the High Court. The Prime Minister was overjoyed when handed a note during Question Time giving him the result of the High Court case. While the NIWG and ATSIC called for a constitutional referendum to ensure that the race power could be used only for the benefit of Aborigines, John Howard offered to fund a test case of his legislation in the High Court. Gareth Evans erupted in the heat of the moment: 'This bloke seems to be never so happy as when he's bashing blackfellas'. Once again the prospect of Senate compromise was slight.

Because the Senate wanted to hold firm on maintaining the right to negotiate for all native title holders, whether their land was vacant crown land or subject to pastoral lease, the government took the line that the Senate 'continues to treat farmers as second-class citizens'. It was doing no such thing. On the last day of debate, the stand-off between the Howard government and the Senate came down to one issue: the right of native title holders to be heard by an independent tribunal before mining proceeded on pastoral leases subject to native title claim.

For the Senate, the bottom line was deciding what was fair for native title holders. There would be no fairness or equity in saying Aborigines would lose all say over mining on their land simply because 50 years ago, without their consent, a pastoral lease was granted over their land which they still occupied. It would be even more unfair to deprive native title holders in the Kimberleys and Cape York from a right to negotiate with a mining company because their traditional land, to which they held title, was under pastoral lease. If States wanted to give pastoralists the same rights with mining companies as enjoyed by native title holders, good luck to them. But the Senate, and Senator Brian Harradine in particular, were not swayed by specious equity arguments to abandon the Commonwealth's responsibility to set a fair and decent bottom line for all native title holders.

As in December 1997, the Democrats and Greens were uncompromising in putting the NIWG amendments, while Brian

Harradine played his enigmatic role. He had set his bottom line with a modest set of 18 amendments to a 364 page Bill. He created the space and maintained the pressure for a government compromise by agreeing to most government proposals. Before lunch on the last day, he had given the government their preferred threshold test and sunset clause. His lawyers, being of the view that in the end it would not be a problem, had constructive discussions with government about the *RDA*. All attention was focussed on the right to negotiate.

Over lunch, the indigenous leaders pulled the plug, with Lois O'Donoghue declaring: 'I've given up on this process. They're just playing Russian roulette with our lives. At the end of the day, we've got our people out there to face. Their perception is that we're in here negotiating away our native title rights'. Harradine was still prepared to cut a deal in the national interest, being anxious to avoid a race election and wanting to obtain the bare minimum he thought achievable for indigenous Australia. Gatjil Djerrkura, Pat Dodson and Peter Yu, who were concerned for their northern constituency, accepted Harradine's commitment to salvage some protection of culture and heritage on pastoral leases. They remained passionately committed to their people's right to negotiate with mining companies, but wanted to avoid a political result whereby traditional communities living and working on pastoral leases in Northern Australia would be denied protection of their cultural heritage by governments intent on taking away their economic bargaining power with mining companies. Other members of the NIWG, such as Geoff Clarke, Aden Ridgeway and Les Malezer (who is from the Brisbane based Foundation for Aboriginal and Islander Research Action), were opposed to any compromise that took away the economic bargaining power of native title holders. They had dropped the bar as low as they could go. Their southern constituencies did not include long-settled traditional communities living and working on pastoral holdings.

Instead of a right to negotiate with mining companies on pastoral leases, native title holders under the Harradine compromise were to be given a right to put their case to an independent State tribunal, which would make a determination which could be overridden by the State premier. This compromise, described as 'the non-exclusive area impact procedure', was designed by the

NIWG/Labor Party QCs Ron Castan and John Basten in co-operation with Harradine's lawyers John McCarthy QC and Jeff Kildea. Labor had joined with Harradine in putting the compromise to the government. As a compromise, it was unofficially supported by some members of the NIWG. Richard Court and Rob Borbidge refused to give Howard the green light. The most they would accept was their own tribunal having the power only to make recommendations to their mines ministers. Howard did not have the political muscle and will to impose a final settlement on his State colleagues. So close and yet so far. This remaining issue had nothing to do with the rights of the pastoralists. Harradine met with Howard five times during the last two days of the second Senate debate. The Prime Minister could not see his way clear to signing off on a principled compromise. Once the deal was off, Harradine revisited earlier sticking points, doing legislative backflips and enacting his personal preferences. The moment for principled and fair compromise had passed. The final Senate Bill would be completely unacceptable to the House of Representatives, yet again. Everyone was preparing for the Queensland election.

8 | THE HOWARD–HARRADINE COMPROMISE 1998

Had *Wik* been resolved by Easter 1998, it would not have been a significant issue in the Queensland election two months later. Going into the State election campaign, Premier Rob Borbidge expected to make political capital out of people's unresolved *Wik* fears. However, every time he played on people's fears about *Wik* during the election campaign, he was trumped by Pauline Hanson's One Nation Party, which espoused an unrealistic one point plan of extinguishment of native title without compensation. Queensland's Labor leader, Peter Beattie, had to soft peddle native title issues and Kim Beazley told his federal colleagues not to mention *Wik* north of the Tweed.

Meanwhile the NIWG was engaged in private discussions with senior National Party officials, such as President Don McDonald, seeking a compromise solution. These talks came to nothing but were a useful indicator of the NIWG's unofficial bottom line, which included a preparedness to trade all economic rights on pastoral leases provided there was an adequate State regime for the protection of culture and heritage. The parties produced a draft agreement which included big picture items such as commitment to a treaty, constitutional entrenchment of Aboriginal rights and a national compensation fund in addition to the Indigenous Land Fund. During these negotiations, McDonald spent $4 million on a new pastoral lease in Queensland subject to native title claim. Presumably he thought his investment safe. Despite more than a year of fear and anxiety in the bush, there had been no adverse effect on property values.

During the Queensland election campaign, influential Liberals, including Tony Abbott and Helen Coonan, were convinced of the need after the election to revisit *Wik* for a third time. Meanwhile Senator Harradine—who predicted at the end of the second Senate debate that the Prime Minister would be back and anxious to reach agreement after the Queensland election—had been working on his compromise package, maintaining his resolute opposition to a double dissolution and his commitment to the non-extinguishment of common law native title rights. Since the end of the second Senate debate, John Howard had continued with the implied threat of a double dissolution disclaiming any responsibility for any racial overtones that might mark such a campaign were *Wik* to remain unresolved. Rejecting the Harradine compromise, he told Parliament at the end of the second debate:

> I reject completely the description constantly used by many in the media that, if the *Wik* bill is the subject of a double dissolution, the next election will be a race election. There will be no race election as far as my government is concerned. We will never embrace the politics of race. We will never seek to exploit a political issue or create a political argument based on race. We do not have in our ranks people who have used racist language. We do not have in our numbers people who have used racist language. It will not be a race election so far as my party is concerned. If those media commentators who continue to loosely and glibly describe it as such had any concern for the harmony of the Australian community, they would stop using such a ridiculous title.

However, his senior Queensland National Party Senator in the Senate, Ron Boswell, discredited such a line in his closing remarks during the second Senate debate when he referred to Gareth Evans' intemperate remark about the Prime Minister's delight in 'bashing blackfellas'. Boswell warned:

> If such a person finds the normal cut and thrust of politics too much, how will candidates new to politics in the heat of an election debate, with native title the big issue, be able to keep from making unhelpful comments? It is tempting to think that all debate in the public arena will be conducted as if it were in this chamber tonight during the committee stage. That debate was mostly restrained, careful and backed up by professional advice on complex issues. But come an election, the committee of the Senate will not be in charge.

Brian Harradine, who had been bending over backwards to find a principled compromise, put the country on notice: 'Any election on this bill would mean the government allowed political ideology to triumph over the national good and national reconciliation.

It is a fearful prospect.' The election of Labor's Peter Beattie and One Nation's good showing in the Queensland election provided the double pincer needed to put pressure on John Howard for further compromise. Harradine knew he would be able to win further concessions in favour of native title holders.

The four sticking points set down by the Prime Minister at the end of the first Senate debate were the focus of everyone's attention. The **six year sunset clause** was always a hollow piece of political symbolism. The South Australian Liberal government had admitted as much in evidence to the parliamentary committee in September 1997. The sunset clause had to go. There was a need for a stricter **threshold test** to weed out conflicting, ambit and spurious claims. Harradine did not want the bar set so high that those claimants whose families had been locked out of pastoral leases would be locked out of the claims process. Harradine accepted that as far as possible any native title legislation should be non-discriminatory. He and his lawyers worked hard to obtain government agreement on a formula of words about the *Racial Discrimination Act* which was workable and sufficiently certain to be acceptable to government.

The major sticking point was **the right to negotiate** with mining companies on pastoral leases. By leaving the decision to the State minister for mines, John Howard claimed at the end of the second Senate debate that he would be giving native title holders the same procedural rights as pastoralists. But he was not. Pastoralists usually enjoy a complete veto over any mining in the vicinity of homesteads or structures used for business, recreation or worship. Harradine ultimately conceded the government's prerogative to take away the added economic bargaining power—which a right to negotiate gave to Aborigines—in the name of equal treatment. Insisting on equal treatment of pastoralists and Aborigines, he then turned the argument back on government. How could you give equal protection to native title holders when the State minister for mines could approve mining even on sites used for residence, business, recreation and worship? There was a need for an impartial transparent process to determine how mining would impact on coexisting native title rights. Though the decision of the court or tribunal could be overridden by government, the decision should be judicially reviewable. The

Labor–Harradine compromise proposal of the second Senate debate was to be the centre piece of any Howard–Harradine compromise in a third Senate debate.

The Prime Minister needed to save face and Harradine needed assurance that the outcome was more favourable to Aborigines on the four key sticking points. Howard had been hostage to Court and Borbidge at Easter 1998. After the second Senate debate, John Howard had said, 'We were always ready to embrace a different way of achieving the objectives we wanted, particularly in the four critical areas'. He had claimed that Brian Harradine 'in the final analysis, wasn't in a very compromising mood'. Third time around, Borbidge disappeared from the political landscape and the Prime Minister realised that a failure to reach agreement with Harradine could cause grave electoral damage to the National Party, with a double dissolution doubling One Nation's chances in the Senate. The key sticking point would remain the right to negotiate.

The week before the Queensland election, I held discussions with persons close to the Prime Minister and carried a message to Senator Harradine, urging that he contact Howard immediately after the Queensland election. After the second Senate debate, Gatjil Djerrkura had said, 'The right to negotiate is an effective means by which native title holders and claimants may seek to ensure protection of significant spiritual and cultural areas.' The Howard government was insistent that any protection of spiritual and cultural areas not permit the native title claimants any economic bargaining power greater than that enjoyed by pastoralists.

Ron Castan's 'non-exclusive area impact procedure' could not be labelled a huge disincentive to mining investment. This compromise would allow a State to remove the right to negotiate with a mining company on a pastoral lease provided the native title claimants had access to a State tribunal making a determination that could be overridden by the government acting in the State interest. This alternative could deliver some minimal protection on pastoral leases but without the added power to negotiate commercial arrangements with mining companies. Unfortunately in its final form, Harradine had to agree to the alternative State procedure being available on lands which were previously subject to pastoral lease even though they were now vacant crown land. This was an unprincipled demand of the Howard and Court governments.

While Prime Minister Howard again entertained the miners and pastoralists to lunch at the Lodge, Senator Harradine decided it was essential to conduct his negotiations in strictest confidence. The details of the compromise were announced on 1 July 1998. The Aboriginal leadership was divided in its response. Noel Pearson was fulsome in his praise of Harradine:

> It looks, on the face of it, in this penalty shoot-out situation, Brian Harradine's won four-nil. Full credit to Senator Harradine for having promised us that he was going to hold the line. He's surely held the line. He's held out on a stubborn position. It appears that Senator Harradine has substantially saved the position that will give Aboriginal people procedural rights on pastoral leases, which from one point of view at least looks like a right to negotiate under a different guise.

Next day, Pearson fell in with other members of the NIWG and condemned the compromise. On 3 July 1998, I, while overseas, endorsed the Harradine compromise, saying, 'Given the political constraints, Brian Harradine delivered for Aboriginal Australia'. Gladys Tybingoompa came back on to the public stage describing Harradine as a 'wobbly dancer'. She felt betrayed and wondered why Harradine had ever danced with her and her people.

On 5 July 1998, Harradine apologised to the Aborigines for their exclusion from the last round of negotiations, saying, 'I was concerned that if others were involved there might be leaks and the horses might be frightened and they'd bolt.' On the day of the apology, Gatjil Djerrkura, Chairman of ATSIC, issued a statement on the Howard–Harradine agreement, which he described as 'an advance on the government's original bill'. Though concerned about the weakening of the right to negotiate, he acknowledged that progress had been made. Still unconvinced about the overall bill, Djerrkura nonetheless praised Harradine for his initiative: 'We suspect Senator Harradine has taken the Prime Minister as far as he could to avoid a race based election. I think he has demonstrated courage and integrity throughout this debate.'

This compromising attitude from ATSIC, Noel Pearson's mixed messages to the public and my endorsement of the Harradine package were too much for Paul Keating, who emerged from retirement to attack Harradine and me. Although I was overseas for the duration of the Howard–Harradine negotiations, I had endorsed the compromise as the best achievable outcome, given Senator Harradine's commitment to avoiding a double dissolution and his self-imposed restrictive role for the Senate as a house of review which should not unduly obstruct the government's legislative program. Keating wrote in the *Sydney Morning Herald*, 'Talk about meddling priests! When Aborigines see Brennan, Harradine and other professional Catholics coming they should tell them to clear out.' He said that Senator Brian Harradine and I had 'saved Howard from paying the price of his folly, and made the Aborigines pay instead.' Keating later claimed the compromise had my fingerprints 'all over it'.

Under the compromise, the Howard government abandoned the sunset clause. Harradine agreed to the government's physical connection test in the registration test but insisted that the stolen generation be accommodated if they could establish that their parents had maintained the necessary connection with the land. The government required that any stolen generation claim for registration be determined by the Federal Court and not the Registrar.

The convoluted lawyers' debate over the *RDA* was resolved with a slight reworking of the Opposition's proposed amendment from the second Senate debate. The note about the relationship between the *NTA* and the *RDA* which had been attached to the clause was made an integral part of that clause, satisfying the government lawyers that the *RDA* could not place in doubt the effect of any past or future action which affected native title and which was valid under any clause of the *NTA*. According to the government, this meant that the *RDA* would operate only on subjects outside the *NTA* and be relevant in construing only ambiguous terms in the *NTA*. The new clause probably operates in the same way as the old clause but the Labor lawyers who wanted a new clause that was not a clause buster were able to save face. The Democrats and Greens remained insistent on a clause buster which would truly subject each clause of the *NTA* to the *RDA*. Labor, despite its resolution at the party conference in January 1998, could not credibly object to the compromise clause.

As in the first Senate debate, Senator Harradine conceded the government's prerogative to redesign the right to negotiate. He succeeded in having the government remove the power of a minister to intervene before the conclusion of the negotiation period. He had to give ground, permitting the removal of the right in town and city areas, and for the development of infrastructure facilities. In these circumstances, there would be guaranteed access to an independent State tribunal to assess the impact of developments on native title.

Harradine also succeeded in securing amendments for the legislative suspension rather than the extinguishment of native title on non-exclusive tenures, in national parks and on government lands not yet in use. The government dropped the provision which would have excluded land from claim simply because it had been transferred from one government department to another. If the land had never been used by the government it could still be claimed.

Harradine insisted that any expanded primary production activity on pastoral leases which interfered with native title be permissible only with the agreement of the native title holders unless the activity could have been authorised on the lease prior to the *Wik* decision. The Western Australian government won an unprincipled concession by moving the relevant date for possible authorisation of primary production activity from the *Wik* decision to 31 March 1998. In the meantime, the Western Australian parliament had expanded the types of activity permitted on pastoral leases, bringing them into line with leases in other jurisdictions.

Nonetheless, the Harradine clause ensures that pastoral leases cannot be used for all classes of primary production. If more intensive primary production requires the grant of a new tenure to the farmer, the farmer would need to negotiate with the native title holders or the native title rights would have to be acquired compulsorily in a non-discriminatory way. If the term of a new pastoral lease is to be longer than the term of an existing lease, government will be required to consult and assess the effects on native title rights. When native title claimants have registered a claim over a pastoral lease, they will enjoy statutory access rights until the determination of the claim and also any additional rights which they can establish in court before a final determination of the claim. If native title holders have a right of exclusive possession over land, farmers will not be entitled to the grant of a licence for an off-farm activity such as grazing if it would interfere with the exercise of native title rights.

If a mining lease is to be renewed for a longer period than the original lease or if it were to confer additional rights, it will have to go through the right to negotiate regime. If a miner and native title claimants fail to reach agreement, the arbitral body will be entitled to consider the economic impact of the proposed development on the claimants and on the local region. Before an exploration company can avail itself of the expedited procedure which bypasses the right to negotiate, the arbitral body will need to consider the effect of the proposed activity on the community and on the social activities of the native title holders. Native title holders will have the same procedural rights as other land holders when public services such as water, sewerage, electricity and telecommunications cross their land.

During the first Senate debate, the Labor Party had written itself out of the script with its 350 amendments, conducting itself as if it were the government. From the sidelines, Labor warned of constitutional challenges and further High Court interventions on native title. These dire warnings lost their political clout with the High Court's decision on Hindmarsh Island at the commencement of the second Senate debate. The warnings sounded very hollow during the third Senate debate after retired Chief Justice Mason made the observation that he had a problem with Labor's claim 'that any winding back of rights previously granted by statute to a particular group and to no others necessarily discriminates against that group'. At the end of the second Senate debate Labor had remained insistent that the right to negotiate with mining companies be exercisable both at the mining and exploration phases. However, Labor had been a key player in the formulation of the compromise alternative to the right to negotiate on pastoral leases. On the eve of the third debate, Harradine told the *Sunday* program:

> Look, if I were Kim Beazley I would have looked at the arrangements that have been reached, and said, look, Mr Prime Minister, I can recognise our own writing in this, thank you very much. And we could have had a unanimous effort to go ahead, instead of all this confusion.

Unless there had been a change of government, Harradine's compromise was the only option for those advocating an enhancement of Aboriginal rights over and above what the Howard government had on offer with its Ten Point Plan. From his first speech during the first Senate debate to his last speech in the second Senate debate, Harradine always expressed grave reservations about the prospect of a double dissolution election in which *Wik* was unresolved.

As an independent Tasmanian Senator, Harradine always took the view that the government is entitled to govern. It is for government to decide issues of workability and certainty, but the Senate is entitled to consider the moral bottom line on key issues, especially the protection of human rights. Given the political constraints, Brian Harradine did deliver for Aboriginal Australia in his closed door negotiations with John Howard. Sadly, government left Aborigines outside the door. And once Queenslanders elected a Labor government, they were left outside the door as well.

Under the compromise, the Howard legislation does not take away the right to negotiate on pastoral leases. It simply allows state governments to do so. By doing nothing, Labor Premiers Peter Beattie and Bob Carr can maintain the right to negotiate on pastoral leases. Once the Harradine compromise was announced, Peter Beattie was unable to commit his government to retention of the Keating right to negotiate. Keating's one time minister Bob Collins said that if Beattie or Bob Carr took away the right to negotiate on pastoral leases, a Beazley government would have no credible ground or argument to restore it. During the third Senate debate Labor declined Harradine's request in the Senate that it commit itself to legislating the Keating right to negotiate back into existence on return to government.

Gladys Tybingoompa felt betrayed by her dancing partner, Brain Harradine, describing him as 'Judas Iscariot that betrayed Jesus in the Garden'. Presumably her sense of betrayal by non-indigenous Australia will be heightened when a State Labor government legislates to take away the right of her people to negotiate with mining companies on land subject to pastoral lease. During the third Senate debate, Labor abandoned its support for their QCs' 'non-exclusive area impact procedure' and recommitted itself to a two-fold right to negotiate, exercisable by native title holders in all circumstances. This commitment at the federal level in opposition could not be matched by Labor at the State level in govenrment.

Kim Beazley joined forces with Peter Beattie explaining the need for a national standard and a national system. They said it would be undesirable to have different rules either side of the Queensland border, and they stressed the problems confronting Premier Beattie with an uncertain majority in the new Queensland Parliament. However, they deliberately overlooked three facts. Aborigines sought a national system for mining applications in 1993; Paul Keating could not deliver it to them because the Goss Labor government and other State governments were adamant that mining applications should be determined by State tribunals and ministers. Half the Aboriginal land in the Northern Territory is subject to veto and not just a right to negotiate. Under the Howard-Harradine compromise, the right to negotiate remains in place until a State takes it away; for Labor to honour its commitment to Gladys Tybingoompa, it need do only nothing.

With the passage of the *Native Title Amendment Act 1998*, all parties can now weed out the conflicting, ambit and overlapping claims in the backlog of 678 cases. There will be greater emphasis on negotiated agreements. Pastoralists are assured that the spirit of the *Wik* decision is written into law. Their rights prevail over any conflicting rights of native title holders. They can engage in primary production in the same way that they could prior to the *Wik* decision. Native title claimants will have a once only right to negotiate with mining companies on vacant crown land outside town and city boundaries. In other circumstances they will have access to an independent tribunal to put their case. They will retain the right to negotiate on pastoral leases until State governments replace that right with a Commonwealth approved regime guaranteeing access to an independent tribunal. Should the Labor States take away the right to negotiate, it is unlikely that a new Commonwealth Labor government would restore it. It is arguable that on this key issue the Howard–Harradine compromise delivered all that any government could have delivered to Aboriginal Australia. After all this compromise enjoyed Labor support during the second Senate debate and Coalition support during the third Senate debate. The only change was the Queensland election result and the altered position of the parties in the opinion polls.

After 109 hours of Senate debate and 314 amendments to Mr Howard's original Ten Point Plan, *Wik* is no longer a national political issue. But the compromise has to be made to work. Aborigines, having been locked out of the final negotiations between Howard and Harradine, cannot be expected to own the outcome as they did in 1993. For the first time since *Mabo*, the Coalition parties have had to put their name to a legislative solution. On the key sticking point—the right to negotiate with mining companies on pastoral leases—the major parties were basically in agreement. All major political parties now accept the principles of non-extinguishment of common law native title rights and non-discrimination in the treatment of common law native title rights. Labor might maintain a commitment to a stronger right to negotiate but it will not campaign on it during an election. Federal Labor might maintain some rhetorical commitment to maintaining a right to negotiate on pastoral leases but it will forgive its State governments for legislating it away for the sake of national consistency and their own political survival. The majority of Aborigines who could never establish a native title claim will still have access to the Indigenous Land Fund, which enjoys bipartisan support and which will reach $1.289 billion by June 2004, permitting annual payments of $45 million for land purchases and land administration.

The last speech in the third Senate debate was delivered by Senator Harradine. He was relieved to have avoided a double dissolution election on *Wik* without sacrificing common law native title rights. He remained convinced that such an election 'would have torn the fabric of our society and set race relations back 40 or 50 years'. He concluded:

> We now have an opportunity to move forward from the bitterness which has divided the nation over the last few years. If we give the amended Native Title Act a chance to work, I am confident that in time indigenous and non-indigenous, country and city, will be reconciled on this issue. The community's recognition of native title after 200 years is not the panacea which some people believe it to be, nor is it the demon that others have tended to characterise it as. It is a crucial aspect of the ongoing process of reconciliation which we must continue to pursue with justice and fairness.

> With these amendments to the *Native Title Act*, we can put in a firm foundation of the future.

Neither John Howard nor Kim Beazley wants to revisit *Wik* in the years ahead. It is now behind us as a major national political issue. The new law has to be made to work on the ground. The Democrats and Greens will continue to enjoy their political niche, advocating the aspirations of the key Aboriginal leaders. One Nation will continue to carve out its niche, espousing the extinguishment of native title and the abolition of all Aboriginal programs, including the Indigenous Land Fund. The major political parties will live with the detailed compromise which was legislation by exhaustion. And the debate will continue whether Brian Harradine let Howard off the hook or seized the moment and delivered the most that was achievable in the name of justice, workability and certainty.

BIBLIOGRAPHY

High Court decisions

Brandy v *Human Rights and Equal Opportunity Commission* (1994–95), 183 *Commonwealth Law Reports* p 245.

Kartinyeri v *The Commonwealth* (1998), 152 *Australian Law Reports* p 540.

Mabo v *Queensland (No 1)* (1988), 166 *Commonwealth Law Reports* p 186.

Mabo v *Queensland (No 2)* (1992), 175 *Commonwealth Law Reports* p 1.

Western Australia v *Commonwealth* (1994–95), 183 *Commonwealth Law Reports* p 373.

North Ganalanja Aboriginal Corporation v *Queensland* (1995), 185 *Commonwealth Law Reports* p 595.

Wik Peoples v *Commonwealth* (1996), 187 *Commonwealth Law Reports* p 1.

Parliamentary Hansard and Reports

Parliamentary Joint Committee on Native Title and the Aboriginal and Torres Strait Islander Land Fund, *Reports 1–11*, Parliament of the Commonwealth of Australia, 1994–98.

First Wik debate in the Parliament

HOUSE OF REPRESENTATIVES
Commonwealth Parliamentary Debates (HofR)
Bill introduced: 4 September 1997 (p 7886)
Debate commences: 25 September 1997 (p 8459)
Bill passes: 29 October 1997 (pp 10011, 10098)
Rejection of Senate amendments: 6 December 1997 (p 12313).
SENATE
Commonwealth Parliamentary Debates (Senate)
Bill introduced: 11 November 1997 (p 8781)
Debate commences: 25 November 1997 (p 9404)
Bill passes: 5 December 1997 (p 10587).

Second Wik debate in the Parliament

HOUSE OF REPRESENTATIVES
Commonwealth Parliamentary Debates (HofR)
Bill introduced: 9 March 1998 (p 781)
Debate commences and passes: 11 March 1998 (pp 923, 974)
Rejection of Senate amendments: 9 April 1998 (p 2937).
SENATE
Commonwealth Parliamentary Debates (Senate)
Bill introduced: 11 March 1998 (p 861)
Debate commences: 1 April 1998 (p 1782)
Bill passes: 8 April 1998 (p 2491).

Third Wik debate in the Parliament

HOUSE OF REPRESENTATIVES
Commonwealth Parliamentary Debates (HofR)
Motion for reconsideration: 3 July 1998 (p 5735)
Debate commences: 3 July 1998 (p 5746)
Bill passes: 3 July 1998 (p 5761)
SENATE
Commonwealth Parliamentary Debates (Senate)
Consideration of message from House of Representatives: 6 July 1998 (p 4165)
Debate commences: 6 July 1998 (p 4194)
Bill passes: 8 July 1998 (p 4365).

Books and writings

ATSIC, *Native Title Amendment Bill 1997: Issues for Indigenous Peoples*, ATSIC, Canberra, 1997.

F Brennan, *One Land, One Nation*, University of Queensland Press, St Lucia, 1995.

B Bunbury, *Unfinished Business: Reconciliation, the Republic and the Constitution*, ABC Books, Sydney, 1998.

Council for Aboriginal Reconciliation, *Proceedings of the Australian Reconciliation Convention*, 5 volumes, Council for Aboriginal Reconciliation, Canberra, 1997 (also available on http://www.austlii.edu.au/car/).

Essays on the Mabo Decision, Law Book Company, Sydney, 1993.

Foundation for Aboriginal and Islander Research Action, *Bringing Australia Together: The Structure and Experience of Racism in Australia*, FAIRA, Brisbane 1998.

H Goodall, *Invasion to Embassy, Land in Aboriginal Politics in New South Wales, 1770–1972*, Allen & Unwin, St Leonards, 1996.

National Indigenous Working Group on Native Title, *Coexistence—Negotiation and Certainty*, NIWG, Canberra, 1997.

H Reynolds, *This Whispering in Our Hearts*, Allen & Unwin, St Leonards, 1998.

MA Stephenson & S Ratnapala, *Mabo: A Judicial Revolution*, University of Queensland Press, St Lucia, 1993.

AE Woodward, Aboriginal Land Rights Commission, *Second Report*, AGPS, Canberra, 1974.

M Yunupingu et al, *Voices from the Land*, 1993 Boyer Lectures, ABC Books, Sydney, 1994.